INTERNATIONAL PERSPECTIVES

ON THE IRISH ECONOMY

INTERNATIONAL PERSPECTIVES

ON THE IRISH ECONOMY

Editor: Alan W. Gray

CONTRIBUTORS:

Kenneth J. Arrow,
Stanford University, California.

Anthony B. Atkinson,
Nuffield College, Oxford.

Michael C. Burda,
Humboldt University, Berlin.

Angel de la Fuente,
Institut d'Anàlisi Economica, Barcelona.

Paul R. Krugman,
Massachusetts Institute of Technology, Massachusetts.

Jeffrey D. Sachs,
Harvard Institute for International Development, Massachusetts.

John S. Vickers,
All Souls College, Oxford.

Xavier Vives,
Institut d'Anàlisi Economica, Barcelona.

First published 1997 by
Indecon Economic Consultants,
Indecon House,
Wellington Quay, Dublin 2, Ireland.

As this publication is part of the
Indecon Public Policy Series
extracts from this publication may be
quoted or reproduced providing
full reference is attributed.

The views expressed in this book
are the responsibility of the
authors and do not necessarily represent
the views of Indecon.

Printed and bound in Ireland
by Colour Books Ltd.

Cover painting: Tony O'Malley, *Gluais*, oil on board, 30" x 48", 1997.
                  Collection of Indecon International Economic Consultants.

Photography for cover by John Kellett
JK
Carborundum prints, based on the painting *Gluais*, by James O'Nolan and James
McCreary of the Graphic Studio Dublin.

Index compiled by Helen Litton

British Library Cataloguing in Publication Data

A catalogue record for this book is
available from the British Library

ISBN O 9531318 O 7

For George and Dorothy, Dorothy and Nico, Norman and Angie

and for Sarah and Caroline, and Emilyrose

Cover

The cover design is of a specially-commissioned painting by Tony O'Malley. Entitled *Gluais* the Irish for 'movement' the work suggests parallels between the impetus for growth and development in the natural world and in the Irish economy.

Tony O'Malley is internationally recognised as one of Ireland's greatest artists. He was invested with the title of Saoi of Aosdána in 1994 by President Mary Robinson. He lives in Callan, Co. Kilkenny with his wife, the artist Jane O'Malley.

Gratitude to the Unknown Instructors

What they undertook to do
They brought to pass;
All things hang like a drop of dew
Upon a blade of grass.

W.B. Yeats

Selected Publications by Alan W. Gray

The Economic Consequences of Peace in Ireland, Indecon Policy Series, 1995

EU Structural Funds and Other Public Sector Investments - A Guide to Evaluation Methods, Gill and MacMillan and associated companies worldwide, March 1995.

Employment Potential in Manufacturing, An Bord Trachtala, The Irish Trade Board, 1994.

Responses to Irish Unemployment - the views of four economists, editor, jointly with Kennedy, K. (ESRI), Walsh, B. (UCD) and McAleese, D. (TCD), Indecon Policy Series, 1992.

"Industry and Trade", in *Ireland and Europe: A Shared Challenge, Economic Co-operation on the Island of Ireland in an Integrated Europe*, Stationery Office, Dublin 1992.

1992 and the Tourism Sector, Europen Bureau, Department of the Taoiseach, Stationery Office, Dublin, 1990, jointly with Scott, Y. (Indecon)

1992 and the Financial Services Sector, Europen Bureau, Department of the Taoiseach, Stationery Office, Dublin, 1990.

"Cost Competitiveness and How to Improve It", in *Competition and Industry, The Irish Experience*, McAleese, D., editor, Gill and MacMillan, 1989.

An Economic Analysis of Petroleum Exploitation Terms in Ireland, the U.K., Norway, Denmark and the Netherlands, Price Waterhouse, 1988, jointly with Kemp, A.G. (University of Aberdeen).

"Seasonality and Other Components in Irish Unemployment Series", *Quarterly Economic Commentary*, The Economic and Social Research Institute, April, 1980, jointly with O'Reilly, L. (Central Bank).

CONTENTS

NOTES ON CONTRIBUTORS

Kenneth J. Arrow

Anthony B. Atkinson

Michael C. Burda

Angel de la Fuente

Paul R. Krugman

Jeffrey D. Sachs

John S. Vickers

Xavier Vives

Kenneth J. Arrow

Kenneth Arrow is Joan Kenny Professor of Economics, Emeritus, and Professor of Operations Research, Emeritus, Department of Economics, Stanford University, California. Professor Arrow is one of the world's most distinguished economists and was awarded the Nobel Memorial Prize in Economic Science in 1972. He holds a MA in Mathematics and a PhD in Economics from Columbia University. He has held senior academic positions in University of Chicago; Massachusetts Institute of Technology; Churchill College, Cambridge; Institute for Advanced Studies, Vienna and Harvard University.

He has been a consultant to the RAND Corporation since 1948 and in 1962 he was Economist with the Council of Economic Advisers, US Government.

Kenneth Arrow is Honorary President of the International Economic Association and was President of the Econometric Society 1956, President of the American Economic Association 1973, and President of the Western Economic Association 1981. He was Co-Chair of Economists Allied for Arms Reduction 1990-1995, First President of the Society for Social Choice and Welfare, Caen, France 1992-1993 and President of the International Society for Inventory Research 1983-1988. He is a Fellow of the Institute of Mathematical Statistics and the American Statistical Association.

He has received over thirty major honours, awards and honorary degrees. These include the John Bates Clark Medal, American Economic Association 1957 and 2nd Class Order of the Rising Sun, Japan 1984.

Anthony B. Atkinson

Anthony Atkinson is Warden of Nuffield College, Oxford. He was previously Professor of Political Economy at the University of Cambridge, and Chairman of the Suntory Toyota International Centre at the London School of Economics. He is a fellow of the British Academy, and is currently President of the Royal Economic Society.

He has been President of the Econometric Society, of the European Economic Association and of the International Economic Association. He has served on the Royal Commission on the Distribution of Income and Wealth, and on the Pension Law Review Committee. He is author of a number of books including *Unequal Shares*, *The Economics of Inequality*, *Lectures on Public Economics* (with J. E. Stiglitz), *Poverty and Social Security*, *Public Economics in Action*, and *Incomes and the Welfare State*.

Michael C. Burda

Michael C. Burda is a professor of economics at the Humboldt University Berlin, and has been a member of the Faculty of Economics and Management Science since August 1993. His research interests are macroeconomics, labour economics and more recently the economic transformation of Eastern Europe.

From 1987-1993 he was an assistant professor and then associate professor of economics at the Institut Europeen d'Administration des Affaires (INSEAD) at Fontainebleau, France.

He received his BA, MA and PhD at Harvard University, Cambridge, Massachusetts, USA. His doctoral dissertation "Essays on the Rise of Unemployment in Europe" was supervised by Professors Jeffrey Sachs and Olivier Blanchard. He has also studied in Göttingen and Kiel.

He was born on April 4, 1959 in New Orleans, Louisiana, USA.

Michael C. Burda is a member of the Council of the European Economic Association, the American Economic Association and the Verein für Socialpolitik. He is the author of a number of scientific articles and the textbook *Macroeconomics: A European Text* (Oxford University Press, now in second edition), which has been translated into German, French, Italian, Spanish and Polish (Russian and Ukrainian translations forthcoming).

Angel de la Fuente

Angel de la Fuente has a PhD in Economics from the University of Pennsylvania, 1991. He is Assistant Professor of Economics, Instituto de Análisis Económico, CSIC, Campus de la Universidad Autónoma de Barcelona. He also holds the position of Associate Professor of the Universidad Autónoma de Barcelona and Research Affiliate of the Center for Economic Policy Research.

He has published in the *Journal of Monetary Economics, Journal of Economic Dynamics and Control* and *Economic Policy*, as well as in numerous Spanish Journals. He is a Member of the editorial board of *Revista Española de Economia and Moneda y Crédito*. His particular research interests are in the areas of growth and regional economics.

Paul R. Krugman

Paul Krugman is Ford International Professor of Economics at MIT. He received his BA from Yale University in 1974, and his PhD from MIT in 1977. From 1977 to 1979 he taught at Yale; then moved to MIT, where he remained on the faculty from 1979 to 1994. He then moved to Stanford from 1994 until 1996. In 1982-3, on leave from MIT, he served as chief international economist of the Council of Economic Advisers.

Krugman is the author or editor of 16 books and more than 200 papers in professional journals and edited volumes. His professional reputation rests largely on work in international trade and finance; he is one of the founders of the "new trade theory", a major rethinking of the theory of international trade. In recognition of that work, in 1991 the American Economic Association awarded him its John Bates Clark medal, a prize given every two years to "that economist under forty who is adjudged to have made a significant contribution to economic knowledge". Krugman's current academic research is focused on the application of ideas from complexity theory and the concept of self-organising systems to economics.

At the same time, Krugman has written extensively for a broader public audience, including a monthly column under the by-line "The Dismal Scientist" for the Internet magazine *Slate*. Some of his recent articles on economic issues, originally published in *Foreign Affairs, Harvard Business Review, Scientific American,* and other journals, are reprinted in his latest book, *Pop Internationalism*.

Jeffrey D. Sachs

Jeffrey Sachs is the director of the Harvard Institute for International Development, the Galen L. Stone Professor of International Trade at Harvard University, and a Research Associate of the National Bureau of Economic Research. He received his BA, *summa cum laude*, from Harvard College, and his MA and PhD from Harvard University. He joined the Harvard faculty in 1980.

Sachs was cited in the *New York Times Magazine* as "probably the most important economist in the world" and in the December 1994 *Time Magazine* issue on 50 promising young leaders as "the world's best-known economist". He has also been a consultant to the IMF, the World Bank, the OECD, and the United Nations Development Programme.

During 1986-1990, Sachs was an advisor to the President of Bolivia, and in that capacity helped to design and implement a stabilisation programme which reduced Bolivia's inflation rate from 40,000 per cent per year to the current rate of 10 per cent per year. In 1989, Sachs advised Poland's Solidarity movement on economic reforms, and at the request of the Solidarity leadership, prepared a draft program of radical economic transformation. From the Autumn of 1991 to January 1994, Sachs led a team of economic advisors for Russian President, Boris Yeltsin. He now heads a non-governmental research unit, the Institute for Economic Analysis, in Moscow.

Sachs is the recipient of many awards and honours, including membership in the American Academy of Arts and Sciences, Harvard Society of Fellows, and the Fellows of the World Econometric Society, He is a member of the Brookings Panel of Economists and the Board of Advisors of the Chinese Economists Society. In 1991 he was honoured with the Frank E. Seidman Award in Political Economy.

John S. Vickers

John Vickers is Drummond Professor of Political Economy at Oxford University and a Fellow of All Souls College. After studying PPE at Oxford (BA 1979), he worked for a while in the oil industry before returning to the university to pursue graduate economics (D.Phil 1985).

From 1984 to 1990 he was Roy Harrod Fellow in the Economics of Business and Public Policy at Nuffield College. He has also held visiting positions at Harvard, Princeton, and the London Business School. He has published numerous journal articles on industrial organisation, privatisation, regulation and competition. His books include *Privatization: An Economic Analysis* (with George Yarrow, 1988) and *Regulatory Reform* (with Mark Armstrong and Simon Cowan, 1994). He was a member of the Hansard Commission on the regulation of privatised utilities, and he is an advisor to Oftel. His current research concerns competition theory and policy.

Xavier Vives

Xavier Vives holds a PhD in Economics from the University of California, Berkeley, 1983. He is Director and Research Professor of Economics at the Institut d'Analisi Economica (CSIC), Campus Universitat Autonoma Barcelona. He also holds the position of Director of the Industrial Organisation Program and is a Research Fellow at the Center for Economic Policy Research. He was a Member of the Council of the European Economic Association 1991-1996, and held the position of Assistant Professor of Economics at the University of Pennsylvania. during the period 1983-1987.

He has published in the main international journals and edited several books. His ongoing editorial functions include the roles of editor of the *International Journal of Industrial Organisation*; co-editor of the *Journal of Economics and Management Strategy*; member of the editorial board of the *Journal of Industrial Economics;* and associate editor of the *Rand Journal of Economics*. He has achieved a number of distinctions which include the award of Premio Juan Carlos I, 1988, for research in social science; Fellow of the Econometric Society, 1992, and Societat Catalana de Economia Prize, 1996.

His research interests include industrial organisation, financial economics and banking, information economics, applied game theory, and European integration.

ACKNOWLEDGEMENTS

I would like to acknowledge first the exceptional work undertaken by the eight economists who have contributed to this unique project. I would also like to thank all of the individuals who have assisted in the planning, implementation and promotion of this publication. It would be hard to overestimate my gratitude to numerous public officials and senior executives of public and private sector companies with whom I have worked over the past number of years and who choose to keep a low public profile while contributing significantly to Irish economic prosperity. Particular thanks are also due to An Taoiseach, Mr. B. Ahern T.D., and to the previous Taoiseach, Mr. J. Bruton T.D., and to staff in the Office of the Taoiseach. Valuable advice on this project was provided by a number of economists in Ireland and internationally particularly Professor D. McAleese, Trinity College Dublin, Professor B. Walsh, UCD and Professor P. Honohan, ESRI. I had excellent assistance with this publication from my colleagues in Indecon (Ireland) including Y. Scott, F. O'Riordan, N. Kelly and N. Cronin. I would also like to thank my friends and Indecon directors Dr. D.S. King and Dr. J. McGuire. A special word of thanks to Dr. L. O'Reilly of the Central Bank of Ireland (who with generosity was my first 'collaborator' in economics), and to D. Palmer. The usual disclaimer applies and the views expressed in this book are the sole responsibility of the authors. I would like to thank Michael Yeats for permission to use the poem by W. B. Yeats *Gratitude to the Unknown Instructors* and to Tony O'Malley for creating the brilliant painting used as the cover of this book.

As always I owe my gratitude to Caroline for inspiration and to Robert and Geoffrey for helping me keep things in perspective.

Alan W. Gray 1997.

Foreword : Irish Economic Challenges and International Perspectives

Alan W. Gray*

1 Introduction

This book is focused on the challenges facing the Irish economy and what can be learned from an international perspective. It considers aspects of three fundamental questions of relevance to Irish policymakers as follows:

> What are the reasons or explanations for the remarkable turnaround in Ireland's economic performance?

> What problems remain to be addressed and what risks are there to maintaining growth?

> What policies should be pursued by the Irish Government?

These issues are addressed in detail in the chapters of this book which include contributions by some of the world's most outstanding economists. This foreword does not pretend to provide an adequate summary of the various contributions but rather attempts to briefly recap on aspects of the three questions outlined above and to also set the context by presenting a brief objective analysis of the recent performance of the Irish economy.

2 Recent Economic Performance

Most of the analysis which has given rise to the Celtic Tiger phenomenon has focused on the growth of the Irish economy and the maintenance of a low inflationary environment. It is important to place this performance in both a historical context for Ireland and in the context of how this performance compares to other countries.

* I am very grateful to Y. Scott for advice and assistance.

2.1 *High Growth*

The recent growth in the Irish economy can be seen from the data in table 1. This shows that the growth in the economy since 1994 has been very rapid by historical standards. While very fast growth rates have been recorded previously (notably in 1989 and 1990) the remarkable feature of recent Irish growth is that it has been sustained at a very high level since 1994. The figures also indicate that the economy has been growing for the last decade although the rate of growth faltered in 1991 in common with most of the industrialised countries.

Table 1 Real GDP in Selected OECD Countries

	Percentage Changes from Previous Period									
	Average		1990	1991	1992	1993	1994	1995	1996	1997[1]
	1970-79	1980-89								
United States	3.5	2.77	1.3	-1.0	2.7	2.3	3.5	2.0	2.4	3.6
Japan	4.6	3.78	5.1	3.8	1.0	0.3	0.6	1.4	3.6	2.3
Germany	2.9	1.79	5.7	5.0	2.2	-1.1	2.9	1.9	1.4	2.2
France	3.5	2.28	2.5	0.8	1.2	-1.3	2.8	2.1	1.5	2.5
Italy	3.6	2.38	2.2	1.1	0.6	-1.2	2.2	2.9	0.7	1.0
United Kingdom	2.4	2.42	0.4	-2.0	-0.5	2.1	3.8	2.5	2.1	3.0
Canada	4.9	3.12	-0.2	-1.8	0.8	2.2	4.1	2.3	1.5	3.5
Total of Above Countries	3.6	2.78	2.5	0.7	1.8	1.0	2.8	2.0	2.3	2.9
Ireland	4.9	3.17	8.4	2.1	4.0	3.1	6.5	10.3	7.3	6.7
Korea	8.8	7.86	9.5	9.1	5.1	5.8	8.6	8.9	7.1	5.3
Mexico	6.4	2.2	5.1	4.2	3.6	2.0	4.4	-6.2	5.1	5.4
Poland	-		-	-	-	-	5.2	7.0	6.0	5.0
Norway	4.8	2.76	1.9	3.1	3.3	2.8	5.0	3.3	4.8	3.8
New Zealand	1.7	2.4	0.3	-2.3	0.6	5.1	5.5	2.7	2.1	2.8
Total OECD	3.8	2.87	2.9	1.0	1.9	1.2	2.9	2.2	2.6	3.0
European Union	3.2	2.24	3.0	1.5	1.0	-0.5	2.9	2.4	1.6	2.3

Source: Derived from *OECD Economic Outlook 61*, June 1997

[1] Projected

Of particular importance is that the average rate of growth since 1994 has been three to four times the average growth of the European Union countries and much higher than the OECD average. The fact that Irish growth rates are higher than for the EU is not particularly remarkable in a historical context. The average growth in real GDP during the 1970s was 4.9% compared to 3.2% for the EU and, since the 1980s, with the exception of 1983 and 1986, Irish growth rates have each year exceeded the EU average. The extent to which recent growth rates have exceeded OECD and EU averages is, however, of significance and in the past couple of years Ireland's growth rate has been the fastest of any OECD country. Ireland's growth exceeded even the Korean economy, which had for the past couple of decades been by far the fastest growing economy in the OECD.

The growth in the Irish economy has been fuelled by a very rapid growth in exports of goods and services. A fast growth in exports has been a feature of the Irish economy for decades, and the growth in exports since 1994 reflects a period of sustained growth in international trade in the OECD and in the European Union. However, as can be seen from table 2 the rate of growth in Irish exports since 1992 has far exceeded the OECD and EU averages. Korean export growth has, however, exceeded even the rapid Irish performance and Irish export growth in the past few years has been outpaced also by Mexico and Poland.

Table 2 Real Exports of Goods and Services

| | Percentage Changes from Previous Period | | | | | | | | | |
| | Average | | | | | | | | | |
	1970-79	1980-89	1990	1991	1992	1993	1994	1995	1996	1997[1]
United States	7.3	5.93	8.5	6.3	6.6	2.9	8.2	8.9	6.5	9.3
Japan	8.6	6.42	6.9	5.2	5.0	1.3	4.6	5.4	2.2	11.0
Germany	5.2	4.68	11.0	12.3	-0.3	-4.9	8.0	5.9	4.9	8.4
France	7.5	3.73	5.4	4.1	4.9	-0.4	6.0	6.3	4.7	7.4
Italy	7.8	3.35	6.8	-0.8	5.9	9.1	10.7	11.6	-0.3	5.3
United Kingdom	5.0	2.97	5.0	-0.7	4.1	3.5	9.2	8.0	6.3	6.0
Canada	5.7	5.33	4.1	1.4	7.6	10.4	14.7	12.0	4.5	7.3
Total of Above Countries	7.3	5.3	7.7	5.3	5.3	2.3	7.8	8.0	4.8	8.8
Ireland	7.5	8.35	8.7	5.3	13.5	9.7	13.6	17.0	10.6	9.4
Korea	21.8	11.62	4.2	11.8	11.0	11.3	16.5	24.0	14.1	15.1
Mexico	8.6	8.09	5.3	5.1	5.0	8.1	17.4	33.0	18.7	16.3
Poland	-	-	-	-	-	-	13.1	18.4	11.2	12.0
Norway	5.8	4.54	8.6	6.1	5.2	3.2	8.2	3.8	8.2	5.7
New Zealand	3.7	3.98	4.5	9.5	2.6	6.0	10.4	2.7	4.5	4.0
Total OECD	7.5	5.66	7.0	5.4	5.4	3.1	8.8	9.0	5.9	8.9
European Union	6.4	4.09	6.4	4.4	3.8	2.1	9.2	7.7	4.6	6.9

Source: Derived from *OECD Economic Outlook 61*, June 1997

[1] Projected

While the growth in exports has undoubtedly fuelled the expansion of the economy, of particular significance is that the growth has been more broadly based with a rapid growth since 1994 (albeit at lower levels) evident in domestic demand. This latter development may not have been given as much attention as it deserves as it has been a critical element in contributing to the increase of tax receipts and the expansion of employment intensive sectors. It is noteworthy that domestic demand has been the element of the Irish economy which has shown very low growth or reductions since the start of the 1980s with the exception of the high growth rates recorded in 1989 and 1990.

Table 3   Real Total Domestic Demand

	Percentage Changes from Previous Period									
	Average									
	1970-79	1980-89	1990	1991	1992	1993	1994	1995	1996	1997[1]
United States	3.2	2.82	0.9	-1.6	2.8	2.9	4.0	2.0	2.5	3.9
Japan	4.5	3.62	5.2	2.9	0.4	0.1	1.0	2.2	4.5	1.4
Germany	2.9	1.36	5.2	4.8	2.8	-1.3	2.8	2.1	0.8	1.3
France	3.3	2.36	2.8	0.6	0.2	-2.2	3.0	1.8	0.8	1.8
Italy	3.2	2.59	2.5	1.8	0.5	-4.5	1.5	2.3	0.2	0.6
United Kingdom	2.3	2.97	-0.6	-3.1	0.2	2.0	2.9	1.5	2.0	3.2
Canada	5.1	3.43	-0.5	-1.2	0.4	2.0	3.1	1.0	1.6	3.9
Total of Above Countries	3.5	2.81	2.2	0.2	1.7	0.9	2.9	2.0	2.3	2.7
Ireland	5.4	0.91	6.5	0.2	0.0	0.7	6.0	5.9	6.8	5.0
Korea	9.0	7.08	13.1	11.3	3.4	4.3	10.2	8.3	7.9	2.5
Mexico	6.5	1.82	7.0	5.7	6.0	1.1	5.5	-13.9	6.5	6.6
Poland	-	-	-	-	-	-	4.6	8.4	12.0	8.0
Norway	3.7	2.11	-0.5	0.8	1.5	3.2	4.4	3.7	2.6	3.8
New Zealand	1.8	2.44	-0.2	-6.2	2.0	5.1	6.1	4.6	3.0	4.1
Total OECD	3.7	2.85	2.9	0.7	1.9	0.9	3.0	2.0	2.8	2.9
European Union	3.1	2.25	2.9	1.4	1.0	-1.8	2.5	2.2	1.3	1.9

Source: Derived from *OECD Economic Outlook 61*, June 1997

[1] Projected

The growth in domestic demand in Ireland since 1994 has been very rapid compared to most other countries and has been a multiple of the average for the OECD or EU. The variability of domestic demand in Ireland since 1980 is significant. It is interesting to note that the desirability of stability of demand at a high level is referred to in the contribution by Arrow to this volume.

2.2 *Improvement in Public Finances*

Perhaps even more significant than the high growth rates for the Irish economy is that this has occurred against a background of a continuing improvement in the Irish public finances and a decline in central government expenditure as a percentage of GDP. The position in relation to the public finances is indicated in table 4. Government expenditure is still, however, at a very high level compared to the East Asian export dependent countries.

Table 4   General Government Financial Balances

	Surplus (+) or deficit (-) as a Percentage of Nominal GDP								
	Average 1980-89	1990	1991	1992	1993	1994	1995	1996	1997[1]
United States	-2.62	-2.7	-3.3	-4.4	-3.6	-2.3	-2.0	-1.6	-1.1
Japan	-1.47	2.9	2.9	1.5	-1.6	-2.3	-3.7	-4.4	-3.1
Germany	-2.09	-2.1	-3.3	-2.8	-3.5	-2.4	-3.6	-3.8	-3.2
France	-2.11	-1.6	-2.0	-3.8	-5.6	-5.6	-5.0	-4.2	-3.2
Italy	-10.98	-11.0	-10.2	-12.1	-9.7	-9.6	-7.0	-6.7	-3.2
United Kingdom	-2.08	-1.2	-2.5	-6.3	-7.8	-6.8	-5.5	-4.4	-2.8
Canada	-4.5	-4.1	-6.6	-7.4	-7.3	-5.3	-4.1	-1.8	-0.2
Total of Above Countries	-2.99	-2.1	-2.7	-4.0	-4.3	-3.6	-3.4	-3.1	-2.1
Ireland	-9.61	-2.3	-2.4	-2.5	-2.5	-1.8	-2.1	-0.9	-1.2
Korea	+1.84	3.7	2.0	1.5	2.8	3.4	4.0	4.0	3.8
Norway	+5.04	2.6	0.1	-1.7	-1.4	0.4	3.3	5.9	6.7
New Zealand	-4.65[2]	-5.4	-4.1	-3.6	-1.2	3.0	3.2	3.1	2.8
Total OECD	-2.94	-2.1	-2.7	-3.9	-4.3	-3.6	-3.3	-2.9	-1.9
European Union	-4.3	-3.8	-4.4	-5.6	-6.5	-5.8	-5.2	-4.4	-3.0

Source: Derived from *OECD Economic Outlook 61*, June 1997

[1] Projected

[2] Average 1986-1989

Not only has the deficit on central government financial balances declined significantly compared to the position during the first eight years of the 1980s but when compared to the trend in other industrialised countries this performance is even more impressive. In 1980 Ireland had a government financial deficit amounting to 12.3% of GDP which was a multiple of that evident for any of the other countries reviewed, while by 1996 the Irish position was much better than the OECD average and was surpassed only by Norway, New Zealand and Korea (the latter country has had surpluses throughout the 1980s and 1990s).

2.3 *Low Inflation*

A key feature of the Irish economic 'miracle' has been the fact that the rapid growth has not resulted in inflationary pressures. Inflation in Ireland has plummeted from the high of over 20% in 1981 to under 2% in 1996. The downward trend in Irish inflation in part reflects the international trend towards lower inflation. For example, UK inflation (which is of particular importance for Ireland, declined from 18% in 1980 to 2.4% in 1996). Interestingly, Irish inflation is lower than that in Korea (5.0%) and contrasts sharply with the high inflation evident in Mexico and Poland (the other countries with very rapid export growth).

Table 5   Consumer Prices

	Percentage Changes from Previous Period								
	Average								
	1970-77	1978-89	1990	1991	1992	1993	1994	1995	1996
United States	6.6	6.19	5.4	4.2	3.0	3.0	2.6	2.8	2.9
Japan	10.6	2.77	3.1	3.3	1.7	1.2	0.7	-0.1	0.1
Germany	5.5	2.97	2.7	3.6	5.1	4.5	2.7	1.8	1.5
France	9.0	7.8	3.4	3.2	2.4	2.1	1.7	1.7	2.0
Italy	12.6	11.78	6.1	6.5	5.3	4.2	3.9	5.4	3.8
United Kingdom	13.9	8.01	9.5	5.9	3.7	1.6	2.5	3.4	2.4
Canada	7.5	6.93	4.8	5.6	1.5	1.8	0.2	2.2	1.6
Total of Above Countries	8.3	5.98	4.9	4.3	3.1	2.7	2.2	2.4	2.2
Ireland	14.0	9.53	3.3	3.2	3.1	1.4	2.3	2.5	1.7
Korea	-	-	8.6	9.3	6.2	4.8	6.3	4.5	5.0
Mexico	14.9	60.52	26.7	22.7	15.5	9.8	7.0	35.0	34.4
Poland	-	-	-	-	-	-	32.2	27.8	19.9
Norway	8.6	8.03	4.1	3.4	2.3	2.3	1.4	2.5	1.3
New Zealand	11.7	12.02	6.1	2.6	1.0	1.3	1.8	3.8	2.3
Total OECD	9.1	9.49	7.2	6.5	5.1	4.4	5.0	5.9	5.4
European Union	10.0	7.56	5.5	5.0	4.4	3.5	3.0	3.0	2.4

Source: Derived from *OECD Economic Outlook 61*, June 1997

The above analysis suggests that the economic growth performance of the Irish economy has been remarkable not only in a recent historical context but also compared to other countries.

3 Explanations for Ireland's Economic Performance

An understanding of the reasons for the remarkable turnaround in the Irish economy is important in attempting to ensure that this growth is maintained. The historical picture shows how easily growth can falter for a small economy such as Ireland. The contributions in this volume represent a unique input to understanding the reasons for the much heralded Irish success.

3.1 *Labour Force Skills and Education*

The analysis presented by Arrow provides a welcome focus on the fundamental reasons for the international successes and failures in economic growth during the past half century. It is particularly important to focus on the underlying bases for economic growth which are often factors not amenable to short term policy initiatives. This is something which is usually lost in political squabbles to gain credit or attribute blame. Arrow draws our attention to the quantity and quality of the supply of labour and the significance of factors such as the retirement age and the nature of child care on this critical resource. He also points to the extreme importance of the quality of secondary-school education and the role of graduate education in facilitating the acquisition of advanced technologies as well as the family environment for child development. Interestingly, the analysis by Krugman also refers to the role of past investments in education in Ireland in leading to the rapid improvements in human capital.

3.2 *Importance of Foreign Investment*

Arrow emphasises the central role of capital formation in economic growth and the role of domestic savings and foreign investment. He highlights the fact that the real gains from foreign investment are improved competitivity and the transfer of knowledge. The role of foreign investment is unusually important for the Irish economy. It is probably not an exaggeration to say that the growth in foreign investment is at the heart of an understanding of the Irish economic miracle. Sachs for example, in his analysis points out that Ireland has in recent years followed a kind of East Asian growth strategy basing rapid growth on manufacturing exports made possible through large inflows of direct investment. Sachs suggests that this growth in foreign investment is related to a favourable rating for Ireland in four crucial dimensions of competitiveness: labour markets, corporate taxation, exchange rate policy and technology transfer via direct investment.

The importance of foreign investment also was highlighted in the contribution by Krugman. Krugman brings us back to the fundamental reasons for Irish growth namely relatively fast productivity growth without a comparable increase in wages. He argues that the big question is why productivity has grown so rapidly and points out that the capital stock grew roughly in line with GDP and (apart from education which was referred to above) dramatic improvements in infrastructure have probably played an important role.

3.3   Shift in Balance of International Trade

Krugman notes that our success is related to becoming the premier European host to inward foreign direct investments and points out that US foreign investment in Ireland is 50% higher per capita than in the UK and 6 times as high as in France or Germany. Of particular value is Krugman's analysis of why Ireland has been so successful in attracting increased foreign investment. A partial answer to this suggested by Krugman is that how nations trade has tilted the balance of geographical advantage in a way that is favourable to Ireland. One part of this is that conventional transportation costs are a steadily less important factor in limiting shipments of goods compared to factors such as delivery time, communication and personal contact. This combined with the fact that market access means that for many industries really long-range, inter-continental trade is still not an option has meant that Ireland's insular location and distance from Continental markets matters much less than formerly. This is related to the growing importance of international trade in services and the increase in the importance of higher value products.

Krugman also outlines some reasons why Ireland has been uniquely successful in taking advantage of what he calls "the changing shape of economic geography". These include the establishment in Ireland of a self-reinforcing industrial cluster, including the impact of classical external economies. Krugman suggests that other factors may have included the demonstration effects of early success as well as the fact that early decisions about the location of investment can produce a cascade of followers. Fuente and Vives in stressing the role of foreign direct investment suggest that the recent growth may be related to the renewed interest by American and other multinational firms in gaining a foothold in Europe and the fact that the fiscal consolidation may have acted as a catalyst, helping to change foreign investors' perception of the country.

3.4 English Speaking Workforce

Ireland is the only country in the European Union apart from Britain which is English speaking. Given the importance of US foreign investment and the question mark which hung over the commitment of the UK to aspects of European integration, this has placed Ireland in a unique position. A number of the contributors to this volume stress the high advantage that comes from the availability of a work force that is not only well-educated but English speaking. This advantage has long been appreciated by business but may not have been given sufficient weight in economic analysis.

3.5 Role of Convergence

One of the explanations for the rate of growth in the Irish economy which may have implications for future growth rates is the issue of convergence. In the contribution by Sachs to this volume he points out that to some extent Ireland's rapid growth is an example of convergence, the empirical regularity in which lower income economies grow more rapidly than the relatively richer economies. Sachs points out that lagging economies such as Ireland have opportunities for "catching up" through the importation of technology and capital and that among the OECD economies in the post-war period the tendency towards convergence has been strong. Sachs, however, notes that something else is also happening in Ireland.

3.6 *Impact of Fiscal Adjustment*

One of the striking features of Irish economic development referred to previously was the fact that the growth occurred at a time of a radical improvement in Ireland's public finances. It appears that this fiscal adjustment assisted growth while in addition the growth contributed to the expansion of tax revenues. In the contribution by Fuente and Vives they suggest that the results of their analysis are consistent with the view that fiscal adjustment was directly responsible for a sizeable increase in the growth as well as the indirect impact on foreign investment referred to previously. Sachs also points out that Ireland's rapid growth was put on course through the dramatic cutbacks in government expenditure as a per cent of GDP beginning in the late 1980s.

3.7 *EU Subsidies*

Ireland has benefited significantly from an inflow of EU subsidies as part of the Commission's objective to facilitate convergence. The contribution to Irish growth of the inflow of large subsidies from the European Union was referred to by Fuente and Vives. These helped finance infrastructure and educational investment without undue pressure on the public finances.

3.8 *Peace in Northern Ireland*

One other factor which is likely to have some impact on the improvement in Irish economic performance, was the 1994 ceasefire in Northern Ireland. While the ceasefire in Northern Ireland did not last (although it has recently been restored) it did contribute to the dramatic increase in Irish tourism and the renewed attention by foreign investors. Some of the benefits for tourism and investment are likely to have remained in the intervening period as a result of increased knowledge of the actual position in Ireland.

3.9 *Partnership Approach to Incomes Policy*

The issue of the partnership approach to income policies is a more debated factor but is likely to have underpinned a number of the other key determinants of Irish growth referred to above.

Fuente and Vives refer to the role of Ireland's relatively low labour costs which have been preserved in recent years by an incomes policy aimed at wage moderation. Krugman also notes that one of Ireland's strong points is that there was enough social cohesion to introduce an effective incomes policy. This social cohesion was also important in underpinning the reduction in the public finance deficits. How to maintain this social cohesion in a context of increasing economic expectations, and the need for a steady reduction in government expenditure to maintain the attractiveness of Ireland as a location for foreign investment will be a major challenge. This will require an increasing focus on equity and fairness in policy determination.

4 Remaining Problems

Despite the remarkable recent Irish economic performance some fundamental problems remain. These include persistently high levels of unemployment and the existence of significant economic poverty. Concerns also remain about the level of competition in the services sector and the appropriate policy towards state-owned industry and utilities.

4.1 *High Unemployment Despite Growth in Jobs*

In table 6 data on employment trends in Ireland are presented. The figures show that the numbers employed in Ireland have increased substantially in recent years. Compared with a net decline in employment trends in the 1980s, there has been growth in employment in each year so far during the 1990s with the exception of 1991. Ireland's recent performance in increasing employment has been substantially better than either the EU or OECD averages.

Table 6 Employment

Source: Derived from *OECD Economic Outlook 61*, June 1997

	1993 Employment (thousands)	Average 1980-89	1990	1991	1992	1993	1994	1995	1996	1997[1]
United States	120,259	1.73	1.3	-0.9	0.7	1.5	2.3	1.5	1.4	2.3
Japan	64,491	1.13	2.0	1.9	1.1	0.2	0.1	0.1	0.5	1.2
Germany	35,215	0.42	3.0	2.5	-1.8	-1.7	-0.7	-0.3	-1.2	-0.9
France	22,226	0.22	0.8	0.0	-0.6	-1.2	0.1	0.9	-0.2	0.2
Italy	20,467	0.17	1.2	0.7	-0.9	-2.5	-1.7	-0.6	0.4	0.0
United Kingdom	25,400	0.58	0.4	-3.1	-2.4	-0.8	0.8	0.8	0.5	1.3
Canada	13,017	2.0	0.6	-1.9	-0.6	1.4	2.1	1.6	1.3	1.8
Total of Above Countries	301,074	1.12	1.4	0.0	-0.1	0.1	0.9	0.8	0.7	1.3
Ireland	1,177	-0.43	4.3	-0.3	0.3	1.5	3.1	4.4	4.0	3.3
Korea	19,253	2.61	3.0	2.9	1.9	1.5	3.0	2.7	2.3	1.2
Mexico	14,354	4.15[2]	1.9	5.5	4.7	4.1	0.9	1.9	5.0	3.0
Poland	14,894	-	-	-	-	-	-1.6	0.9	0.8	1.3
Norway	2,004	0.77	-0.9	-1.0	-0.3	0.0	1.5	2.1	2.7	1.6
New Zealand	1,496	0.13	0.9	-1.4	0.4	2.0	4.3	4.7	3.4	1.7
Total OECD	435,322	1.17	1.6	0.3	0.0	0.1	0.9	1.1	1.0	1.3
European Union	146,004	0.4	1.5	0.0	-1.6	-1.8	-0.3	0.5	0.1	0.4

Percentage Changes from Previous Period

[1] Projected

[2] Average 1988-1989

Despite the strong growth in employment the rate of unemployment remains at persistently high levels. The figures in table 7 show that unemployment rates in Ireland in 1995 remained at 12.2%, much higher than in the UK or in many other industrialised countries. This compares to rates of only 3.1% in Japan, 5.5% in the United States and an OECD average of 7.5%. In the analysis undertaken by Burda it is pointed out that the extent of divergence of labour market performance in Ireland and the UK in terms of unemployment rates is somewhat puzzling, given the extensive economic integration between the two economies.

Table 7 Standardised Unemployment Rates

	Per Cent of Total Labour Force						
	Average 1976-89	1990	1991	1992	1993	1994	1995
United States	6.99	5.6	6.8	7.5	6.9	6.0	5.5
Japan	2.37	2.1	2.1	2.2	2.5	2.9	3.1
Germany	5.24	4.8	4.2	4.6	7.9	8.4	8.2
France	7.89	8.9	9.4	10.3	11.7	12.3	11.6
Italy	8.79	10.3	9.9	10.5	10.2	11.1	12.2
United Kingdom	8.76	6.9	8.8	10.1	10.4	9.6	8.7
Canada	8.85	8.1	10.3	11.3	11.2	10.3	9.5
Total of Above Countries	6.32	5.7	6.4	7.0	7.2	7.0	6.7
Ireland	15.87[1]	13.3	14.7	15.5	15.6	14.1	12.2
Korea	-	-	-	-	-	-	-
Mexico	-	-	-	-	-	-	-
Poland	-	-	-	-	-	-	-
Norway	2.46	5.2	5.5	5.9	6.0	5.4	4.9
New Zealand	5.15[2]	7.7	10.3	10.2	9.4	8.1	6.3
Total OECD	6.72	6.1	6.8	7.5	8.0	7.9	7.5
European Union	8.25	8.1	8.5	9.4	10.9	11.3	11.0

Source: Derived from *OECD Economic Outlook 61*, June 1997

[1] 1983-1989

[2] 1986-1989

4.2 *Poverty and Widening Wage Dispersion*

Despite the growth in the economy, economic poverty remains a significant problem. The detailed analysis presented by Atkinson suggests that poverty touches at least 1 in 10 of Irish households. Poverty in Ireland may be less than in some Member States of the European Union, but it is above that in Northern Europe. Available evidence suggests also that wage dispersion has been widening in Ireland. Earnings of the lowest decile have strengthened while those on top incomes have been rising. The ratio of earnings of the top decile to the bottom decile has grown from 4.2 to 4.9 over recent years.

Table 8 Distribution of Earnings in Ireland

Hourly earnings of employees as a per cent of median earnings

	1987	1994
Bottom decile	47.1	46.5
Top decile	196.1	225.9
Ratio of top to bottom decile	4.2	4.9

Source: Nolan and Hughes, 1997, quoted in *OECD Economic Surveys Ireland* ,1997

5 Risks

In addition to the existing remaining problems there are also a number of risks to continued growth in the Irish economy. The rapid growth in the economy has only existed since 1994 and the recent history of the economy over the past couple of decades shows how fast Irish growth can falter.

One of the risks which exist is potential labour and skill shortages in the economy. Krugman highlights the possibility that at some point Ireland will begin to run up against the constraints of limited labour supply. The number of individuals participating in apprenticeships has increased dramatically in Ireland, but this in itself does not indicate that problems will not emerge. Indeed, there is some evidence that skill shortages are already emerging and action is being taken by the development agencies to prevent this factor acting as a constraint.

Ireland is vulnerable also to a shift in technology. Krugman for example, suggests that changes in technology might vitiate the advantages of a European location which has been a critical factor in determining the growth in foreign investment. Perhaps of even more importance is the risk pointed out by Krugman that some of the Eastern European countries which have large numbers of technically trained people, available at very low wage rates, could mean that other European locations may begin to compete more effectively for foreign investment. Krugman refers also to the issue of Ireland's role within Europe and notes the possibility that EU policies on wages or taxation could damage Ireland's role as an export platform for non-European firms serving the European market.

Sachs refers to risks involving foreign direct investment and points out that countries competing for export oriented investment are in a tough market in which footloose industries searching for cost advantages can choose among many alternative locations. Sachs points out that Ireland's high growth is far from secure in the long term and risks identified by Sachs include a failure to reduce gradually the burden of Government expenditure and taxation. The indirect impact of this on the attractiveness of Ireland for foreign investment could be important.

Another critical risk concerns the maintenance of costs competitiveness. Sachs points out that in the past Ireland has used exchange rate devaluations to restore cost competitiveness at times when domestic costs got out of line. If Ireland joins a single currency, it will close the door on exchange rate flexibility as an instrument of policy. Sachs suggests that it is surely a big risk for a small country that is dependent on export led growth and that perhaps this is even too great a risk. In such circumstances, the need to take other measures to address our relative competitive position gain a new urgency.

6   What Policies should be Pursued?

Given the recent performance of the Irish economy a key issue is what policies should be pursued by the Irish Government to increase the probability that the growth will be sustained and to alleviate the problems which remain. Five areas of policy merit particular attention as follows:

- Long term development measures and structural adjustments
- Responses to Irish poverty
- Labour market reforms
- Regulation and competition policy
- Maintaining the attractiveness of Ireland for foreign investment.

6.1 *Long term Development Measures and Structural Adjustments*

There are a wide range of long term development measures and structural adjustments required in the Irish economy which will be of fundamental importance if Ireland is to reach its productive potential. These areas are often not amenable to quick or easy solutions but will be of critical importance. A number of contributors to this book highlight specific suggestions for aspects of such policy. One area highlighted in a number of contributions is the importance of education. There are two aspects of education which deserve particular mention. The first is how to ensure the maximum participation in secondary level and how to finance and encourage appropriate participation in third level education.

Arrow makes the judgement that virtually universal secondary education is a priority but after that an appropriate increase in university education with adequate emphasis on science and technology, seems to be very important in increasing national output. He points out that graduate education plays a special role in facilitating the acquisition of advanced technologies. On the thorny question of financing higher education, Arrow notes that though the amounts involved are not so great, because of income redistribution reasons, the best system may be to have the costs of a university education repaid by students in subsequent years possibly by an additional small percentage increase in the income taxes of those whose university education was paid for by the state. Apart from education, other aspects of labour skills require ongoing policy attention. Some suggestions are made elsewhere on how to respond to this problem.[1] As well as effective training and skill development initiatives, the appropriate response is also likely to require the attraction of skilled employees from other countries.

---

[1] See Gray, 1997.

Another important long term development issue concerns the longevity of the population and its implications for the use of productive resources and the financing of pensions. Because of an understandable desire for increased leisure time and a perhaps misplaced belief that the total number of jobs is, in a sense, a fixed quantity, 'early retirement' has become more and more frequent. In some cases this has been in response to over-manning levels in certain companies and may perhaps also reflect a mistaken 'ageism' in the workforce. The impact of the loss of experienced skills, and the potential dramatic implications for pensions of this development, has not been given sufficient attention in Irish public policy. Interestingly, Arrow expresses a strong belief that retirement age has to rise (rather than fall) in order to provide more output to sustain the increasing costs of retirement pensions.

The issue of research and development is often raised as a critical development issue particularly for a country such as Ireland which is so dependent on high-tech foreign industry. It is important to stress that it is essential that any investment in research and development is cost effective and significant funds could easily be wasted on low quality or inappropriate research. The focus must be placed on research which is relevant to Irish economic development. Arrow points out that knowledge elsewhere is not made useful to Ireland automatically; it takes effort and understanding. Among factors highlighted by Arrow is the presence of scientists and technologists who are up-to-date with new developments elsewhere. It is, however, important that Ireland takes account of the reality that larger countries with strong research infrastructures have an advantage that in general cannot be overcome. Based on this fact Arrow suggests the merits of taking advantage of sources of comparative advantage, such as lower wages for equally qualified labour, to produce products that are not at the very edge of new quality but have become standardised commodities; and securing individual niches which have not been exploited abroad.

6.2 *Responses to Irish Poverty*

Ensuring that the benefits of Irish economic success reach the poorest sections of our society is a key objective for Irish policy. How to achieve this in the most effective way and with minimum distortionary impacts is a major challenge.

Atkinson in his contribution to this volume suggests that he does not consider means-testing the way forward. In his view, we need to combine elements of 'old' in the form of social insurance, which is the backbone of the social transfer system in all European countries, and 'new' in the form of a participation income, which is a conditional citizen's income.

Atkinson suggests that it is a mistake to see basic income as an *alternative* to social insurance and it is more productive to see it as complementary. What is proposed is a radical scheme which would replace tax allowances, although retaining an earned income disregard, but would keep the existing structure of social insurance benefits. This would represent a partnership between social insurance and basic income and would be an alternative conception of the basic income.

Of particular significance is the Atkinson proposal that a basic income should be conditional on *participation*. The way in which this participation requirement would be defined requires detailed consideration, but qualifying conditions proposed by Atkinson would include (a) work as an employee or self-employed, (b) absence from work on grounds of sickness, injury, or disability, (c) being unemployed but available for work, (d) reaching pension age, (e) engaging in approved forms of education or training, and (f) caring for young, elderly or disabled dependants. The proposed condition is not confined to *paid* work; it is a wider definition of social contribution.

Atkinson proposes also that reducing poverty should become an explicit object of policy. He suggests there should be a poverty criterion, which governments accept as a commitment, and there should be an official *Poverty Report* assessing how far the target has been reached. An effective response to poverty must also consider ways of reducing Irish unemployment.

6.3 *Labour Market Reforms*

The rapid growth in the Irish economy without a dramatic impact on the unemployment rates is a reflection of structural problems in the Irish labour market. There are a number of changes required to address this matter.[2] It is essential that there is a reversal of the rising pattern of taxation on labour. The issue of taxation is discussed in more detail in the analysis on the requirements to maintain the attractiveness of Ireland for foreign investment. From an employment perspective it is, however, important to ensure that tax reductions alter the incentive for individuals to take up job offers. This means that a particular focus of tax reform and other initiatives, should involve removing lower income groups from the tax net, and targeting special tax reductions on those groups likely to be affected by employment/fiscal traps. Other changes are also required to improve the position of the lower income earners, many of whom are not impacted by overall tax changes.

In the contribution by Burda he suggests that it is worth reflecting on the necessary conditions for eliminating structural labour market rigidities in Ireland. He points out that the recent rapid growth of the Irish economy without a corresponding significant impact on unemployment rates indicates a structural problem, which, while without immediate social consequences, might portend the emergence of a two-class society - those with jobs and those without - as has been the case in many other continental European countries.

Burda refers also to the existence of an 'unemployment trap' in Ireland which is an important factor determining labour supply, especially for unskilled, low-wage earners. This refers to the fact that the work decision involves the foregoing of so many benefits that the effective tax rate on labour income can exceed 100%. This applies especially to families in which both adults are unemployed and has already been recognised in policy initiatives in Ireland as a factor which required adjustment.

---

[2] For example, see Gray, 1992.

Arrow stresses the fact that flexibility in the labour market is important to allow labour to flow from declining to rising industries. He suggests that the price of this flexibility should not, however, fall on the workers; to avoid this, adequate unemployment compensation or other social safety nets are needed.

6.4 *Regulation and Competition Policy*

Appropriate regulation and competition policies will play a role in maintaining the growth in the Irish economy. One aspect of this which requires consideration relates to the issue of privatisation. The merits or otherwise of privatisation are significantly influenced by whether firms are operating in competitive or monopolistic markets. This fact is too often overlooked by those for whom policy is determined on an ideological basis rather than on an analysis of the likely consequences. Without appropriate regulation a private sector monopoly is usually much less desirable than a public sector monopoly. The critical importance of competition would suggest that introducing competition may well be a much more important policy priority in improving economic welfare than changing public to private ownership.

In cases, however, where competitive markets exist it is likely that private ownership would be more desirable in terms of economic efficiency. This is in part because the management of such firms is likely to face more stringent budgetary targets and is likely to have much stronger incentives to perform. Another factor is that private sector firms will not be subject to direct political interference or by assumed or actual political constraints on commercial decisions. A shortage of capital arising from government public finance objectives and the fact that civil servants are understandably reluctant to risk taxpayers' funds can also lead to a lack of investment by state owned firms. Some state owned firms may not be able to develop independently because of a lack of scale in circumstances where global competition has in many sectors resulted in increasing economies of scale.

Vickers, in his contribution also points out that the economic arguments in favour of private ownership of firms in competitive markets is supported by the empirical evidence. This leads Vickers to recommend that Ireland should consider early privatisation of its public industries which operate in competitive markets including Aer Lingus, ACCBank, ICC and the TSB.

Where privatisation is considered it is important to pursue a policy which ensures fairness and the avoidance of inequitable distributional impacts which otherwise would result in a benefit to wealthy individuals or companies at the expense of the taxpayer. There can be no economic argument for 'golden circles' or for selling public firms below their market value. In his contribution Vickers recommends that Ireland should pursue privatisation sales methods that ensure that the extent of underpricing is no more than modest (except perhaps in the case of employees of the firms in question). This may suggest the merits of selling a firm in two or more stages which would enable more accurate pricing and by introducing competitive tendering among prospective purchasers. This should apply even in cases where strategic alliances are considered although in such circumstances a more restrictive tendering process may be appropriate.

For firms with market power which usually includes the utilities, the consequences of a shift from public to private ownership is much more complex. Vickers supports this view and suggests that in contrast to the competitive market case it would appear that no general claim can be made as to the economic desirability of privatising firms with market power. Vickers argues that in such cases the accompanying regimes of regulation and competition policy are crucial determinants of the consequences of their privatisation and that this is consistent with the mixed empirical evidence comparing efficiency under public and private ownership.

This raises the issue of the appropriate form of regulation. The regulation of firms with market power particularly in the transport, energy and communications sectors is one of the most challenging tasks facing Irish policymakers, and in many cases is much more important than the issue of public or private ownership. Much of this responsibility falls on the Department of Public Enterprise and the decisions which will be made on regulatory reform in Ireland over the next five years or so are among the most important policy decisions facing the country. Vickers suggests that the keys to successful regulatory reform are adherence to the maxim 'competition where possible, regulation where necessary' and independent economic regulation.

In deciding on the form of regulation of utilities and other firms with market power, the economic objectives are fairly straight forward, namely to ensure that profits are neither excessive nor inadequate and that there are incentives for efficiency and to undertake necessary long term investments. Precisely how to achieve these objectives is a very difficult challenge for Irish policy makers. Vickers interestingly recommends that the best way forward for Ireland may be price cap regulation through a form of rate-of-return regulation with long lags. He suggests that this would provide a price control framework with better incentives than rate-of-return regulation as traditionally practised and is also superior to explicit profit-sharing schemes.

In attempting to apply appropriate regulation or competition policies there is no end to the range of arguments which will be used to suggest why such policies should not be implemented in Ireland. Some arguments such as the strategic importance of the sector are clearly the last refuge of those who have no other defence. Others such as public service obligations have more validity but as Vickers argues there should be scepticism about disapplying competition rules for the sake of public service obligations or the protection of cross subsidies. Vickers points out this is not because public service obligations, or even cross subsidies, are bad, but because monopoly is usually an inferior way of financing them.

The significance of competition was also noted in the contribution by Arrow. Arrow points out that in a small country, it can easily happen that there are too few firms in an industry to permit adequate competition. He highlights the fact that competition is important partly to reduce markups and therefore increase consumer welfare but even more importantly to create a steady pressure for efficiency. Ensuring that regulatory policies foster competition, and where competition is not adequate provide an incentive for on-going efficiency is a policy area where significant developments in Ireland will be required. One area where it is recognised that further improvements are necessary relates to competition in services in Ireland. Barriers to entry or other obstacles to effective competition in Irish services can no longer be accepted.

6.5 *Maintaining the Attractiveness of Ireland for Foreign Investment*

Maintaining the attractiveness of Ireland as a location for foreign investment will be an essential rather than an optional element of policy if growth is to continue. This will require action in the following areas:

- taxation
- infrastructure
- cost competitiveness.

The issue of tax reform and the overall reduction in the level of taxation will be important in maintaining the attractiveness of Ireland as a host location for foreign investment. This will require that Ireland wins the argument in any EU or OECD debate concerning the co-ordination of corporate tax rates. It will also have implications for government expenditure, and the possible adjustments required to compete with other potential locations may be much greater than currently realised. For example, it is somewhat daunting to note that as Sachs points out the top marginal income tax rate in Singapore is 30% and in Hong Kong is just 20%. Sachs also highlights the fact that there are no payroll taxes in Hong Kong or Singapore, and pension contributions are in the form of mandatory payments to individualised savings accounts rather than taxes for government revenue. This kind of individualised provident fund system is also in operation in Malaysia. This would suggest that the Irish Government should consider how to significantly reduce the overall taxation on income beyond what is currently planned. This examination should focus on potential savings in current government expenditure and potential increases in equitable and 'politically saleable' property and capital taxation. There is also a need for a radical examination of how to reduce the exchequer costs of rising pension expenditures. The Government should establish a high level task force to consider the recommendation by Sachs to explore mechanisms for state-regulated private pensions, such as the state-managed systems of mandatory household savings which operate in Singapore and Malaysia and should also consider the concept outlined by Arrow in this volume, of increasing the retirement age.

In addition to making steady progress to reduce income and other relevant taxation, Ireland must make further improvements in its infrastructure. Sachs points out that Ireland rates poorly in international surveys on the quality of infrastructure compared to the most developed economies. While there have been dramatic improvements in Ireland's infrastructure supported by EU funds, some gaps remain and Ireland will need to adjust in the future to the requirement for on-going investment in infrastructure to be funded with reduced levels of assistance from the European Union.

A final area which will be essential if Ireland is to maintain its attractiveness for foreign investment relates to cost competitiveness. The importance of cost competitiveness has somewhat gone out of fashion in some quarters in Ireland, in part reflecting the current favourable position in relation to many areas of costs. While the importance of developing non cost competitive advantages where possible is clear, maintaining our cost competitiveness remains an essential policy requirement and is likely to become more intensive as we face new competitors for foreign investment from Eastern European countries. This is particularly the case given that if Ireland joins the single currency, we will lose the ability to use exchange rate policy to attempt to counter a loss in competitiveness.

Krugman highlights that a threat to Ireland's prosperity lies in the possibility that other European locations may begin to compete more effectively for the role of export platform. He notes in particular that some of the Eastern European countries have large numbers of highly technically trained people, available at very low wage rates. Sachs also stresses the fact that Ireland must maintain cost competitiveness, with changes in wage levels appropriately reflecting changes in productivity and world demand for Ireland's products. Cost competitiveness also requires on-going adjustments to taxation as referred to above as well as policies to encourage increased competition in a wide range of services. Some of the competition and regulatory policies required were addressed above.

7 Conclusion

Ireland is akin to a very small sailing boat on the turbulent seas of the international economy. We have been making exceptional progress in catching up with some larger boats which started earlier on the journey of industrialisation. We have few natural advantages apart from our skills in this ever more difficult race towards economic prosperity. If we are blown off course due to swells on the international economy as has happened on previous occasions this would be unfortunate. If, however, we falter due to disagreements among the crew or self imposed policy mistakes (as has also happened in the past) this would be unforgivable. It is hoped that this book will in some very small way help to reduce the prospect of such an outcome.

References

Bacon, P., 1984, "National Planning", *Irish Banking Review*, June 1994, pp. 3-11.

Barrett, S.D., 1989, "Measuring Poverty in Ireland: An Assessment of Recent Studies", *Economic and Social Review*, 20(4), pp. 353-60.

Baker, T., J. Fitzgerald and P. Honohan, 1996, *Economic Implications for Ireland of EMU*, The Economic and Social Research Institute, Dublin.

Callan, T., 1997, editor, *Income Support and Work Incentives: Ireland and the UK*, Economic and Social Research Institute, Dublin.

Callan, T. and J. Fitzgerald, 1989, "Price Determination in Ireland: Effects of Changes in Exchange Rates and Exchange Rate Regimes", *Economic and Social Review*, 20 (2), pp. 165-188.

Durkan, J., 1992, "Social Consensus and Incomes Policy", *The Economic and Social Review*, 23(3), pp. 347-363.

Fingleton, J., 1997, "Standards of Competition in the Irish Economy", *Journal of the Statistical and Social Inquiry Society of Ireland*, forthcoming.

Geary, P., 1997, "Can Better Contracts Help Solve Ireland's Sterling Dilemma?", *Irish Banking Review*, Summer, pp. 31-43.

Giavazzi, F. and M. Pagano, 1990, "Can Some Fiscal Contraction be Expansionary: Tales of two Small European Countries", in D. Blanchard and S. Fischer, editors, NBER, *Macroeconomics Annual 1990,* MIT Press, Cambridge, MA.

Gray, A.W., 1997, "Challenges for Ireland in the Integrated European Union", in F. O'Muircheartaigh, editor, *Ireland in the Coming Times, Dr. T.K. Whitaker Festschrift*, Institute of Public Administration, forthcoming, Dublin.

Gray, A.W., 1992, editor, *Responses to Irish Unemployment, the views of four economists*, Indecon, Dublin.

Guiomard, C., 1995, *The Irish Disease and How to Cure It, Common-Sense Economics for a Competitive World*, OAK Tree Press, Dublin.

Harrison, M. and P. Walsh, 1994, "A Flow Analysis of the Link between Irish and British Unemployment", Trinity Economic Papers, Technical Paper no. 5, Dublin.

Honohan, P., 1992, "Fiscal Adjustment in Ireland in the 1980s", *Economic and Social Review*, 23 (3), pp. 285-314.

Honohan, P., 1992, "The Links between Irish and UK Unemployment", *Quarterly Economic Commentary*, ESRI, Spring, pp. 33-44.

Keating, W., 1995, "Measuring Growth", in *Proceedings of the Conference on Measuring Economic Growth*, Central Statistics Office and Irish Economic Association, Dublin.

Kinsella, R., 1992, *The Medium-Term Development of Indigenous Industry: The Role of the Financial Sector*, Report for the Industrial Policy Review Group.

Lee, J.J., 1990, *Ireland 1912-1985: Policies and Society*, Cambridge University Press.

Lee, J.J., editor, 1984, *Reflections on Ireland in the EEC*, Irish Council of the European Movement, Dublin.

Leddin, A. and B. Walsh, 1997, "Economic Stabilisation, Recovery and Growth, Ireland 1979-1996", *Irish Banking Review*, Summer, pp. 2-17.

Martin, J., 1996, *Measures of Replacement Rates for the Purpose of International Comparisons, A Note*, OECD Economic Studies, no. 26, Paris.

McCarthy, C. and P. Tansey, 1995, *Taxes on Labour in Ireland and the United Kingdom*, IBEC, Dublin.

McAleese, D., 1997, *Economics for Business*, Prentice Hall Europe, Hemel Hempstead.

McAleese, D., 1990, "Ireland's Economic Recovery", *Irish Banking Review*, Summer, pp. 18-32.

Neary, J.P., 1995, "Factor Mobility and International Trade", *Canadian Journal of Economics*, 28 (4), pp. 4-23.

Nolan B. and G. Hughes, 1997, *Low Pay, the Earnings Distribution and Poverty in Ireland, 1987-1994*, The Economic and Social Research Institute, Dublin.

OECD, 1997, *Economic Survey of Ireland*, OECD, Paris.

OECD, 1997, *Economic Outlook 61*.

O'Hagan, J.W., 1995, *The Economy of Ireland: Policy and Performance of a Small European Country*, Macmillan, Basingstone.

O'Leary, J., 1996, "Some Economic Implications of EMU", Paper presented at the Dublin Economics Workshop, Kenmare.

O'Malley, E. and S. Scott, 1994, "Profit Outflows Revisited", in S. Cantillon, J. Curtis and J. Fitzgerald, editors, *Economic Perspectives for the Long-Run*, The Economic and Social Research Institute, Dublin.

Tansey, P., 1995, "Tourism a Product with Big Potential", in M. D'Arcy, and T. Dickson, editors, *Border Crossings, Developing Ireland's Island Economy*, Gill and MacMillan, Dublin.

Walsh, B., 1996, "Stabilization and Adjustment in a Small Open Economy: Ireland, 1979-95", *Oxford Review of Economic Policy*, 12 (3), pp. 74-86.

Walsh, B., 1992, "Appropriate Policy Changes", in A.W. Gray, editor, *Responses to Irish Unemployment*, Dublin.

Economic Growth Policy for a Small Country

Kenneth J. Arrow
Stanford University, California

1 Introductory Remarks

The following observations are not based on any detailed knowledge of the Irish economy[1] and cannot serve as the basis of specific policies. They are rather very generally drawn from economic theory and from broad observations on the successes and failures in economic growth in the world during the past half-century.

I will, somewhat arbitrarily, classify the factors making for economic growth into two categories. The first are the fundamental resources which determine the production potential of the economy. These change over time in ways partly uncontrollable and partly under the influence of policy. The resources determine the physical possibilities, but other factors determine whether the economy will reach its potential limits. I will in turn classify these limiting factors into two classes, those relating to institutions and those relating to macroeconomic stability.

2 Productive Resources

The maximum potential output of an economy is determined at any given moment by its ultimate resources. These are usually classified as natural resources (e.g. land, minerals), labour, and physical capital (structures and machines). But the output that is made possible by these resources is necessarily determined by the knowledge available in the economy. At different times and in different countries, very different outputs are obtained with very much the same inputs.

---

[1] For specific data about the Irish economy, I am indebted to Alan W. Gray.

1

Projections of potential output then depend ultimately on the changes in the supply of these four categories of resources.

2.1 *Natural Resources*

Though the availability of natural resources is certainly a major factor in many economies, it is much less of an issue in Ireland. Land is the most important natural resource in Ireland. Land in general is constant in supply over time. Its productivity may change, but that comes under the heading of changes in knowledge. Other currently utilised natural resources in Ireland include marine and fishing resources and zinc deposits.

2.2 *Labour*

The supply of labour is, on the contrary, subject to great variation in both quantity and quality. The quantity will change as a result of several factors.

(a)   Age distribution: Specifically, the proportion of the population in the working ages limits the amount of labour for a given population. The rest of the population are either children, not yet in the labour force, or retired. This proportion varies in well-known though complicated ways according to the variations in birth and mortality rates. Both are falling everywhere, though in very different proportions.

(b)   Labour force participation: Even among those of working age, not all work. An especially variable part of the labour force is the participation of women. This has been rising everywhere in the advanced world including Ireland, though the level of female participation in Ireland is still below the European level (48% as compared with 57%).

These two variables are important for forecasting. They are to some extent affected by policy variables, for example, the age of retirement in social security systems, the school-leaving age, child care for pre-school children (to facilitate their mothers' working), and child subsidies, usually through the tax system. Certainly retirement age and child care can have

2

considerable significance. The others are more doubtful in their effects. I personally strongly believe that retirement age has to rise to provide more output to sustain the increasing costs of retirement pensions due to increases in longevity. People are not only living longer but also are healthier and can contribute more to society's output.

The quality of the labour force is of even greater importance in the economic development of a country and especially in determining *per capita* output.

(c)   Education: Repeated studies have shown the importance of education in increasing individual productivity. Some studies even claim that all international variations in labour productivity can be explained by two factors, educational level of the labour force and capital per worker. I think this is exaggerated, as will be discussed below under the heading of institutions. But there is no question of the extreme importance of achieving a very high level of secondary-school education. Undoubtedly, the quality of the education also matters, but surprisingly little is known about the relation between educational quality and productivity. Ireland has 93% of all its 16-year olds in secondary education, and OECD figures indicate that Ireland has a good achievement in mathematics and science at the eight grade.

To judge by trends in the United States, the wage gap (and by inference the productivity gap) between secondary-school and university graduates is widening rapidly (after having fallen in the 1960s). Since the proportion of university graduates in the work force has been growing, this increased gap is especially surprising. The usual argument is that new developments in technology have put a greater premium on university training in the job market.

The proportion between secondary and university education has to be looked at carefully. Some countries (India being a notable example) have a very disproportionate investment in universities. This reflects a very inegalitarian society. Nevertheless, it is clear that universities are now moving into a more important role in increasing labour productivity than they have in the past. In my judgement, virtually universal secondary education is a priority, but after that an appropriate increase in university education, with adequate emphasis on science and technology, seems to be very important in increasing national productivity. Graduate education plays a special role in facilitating the acquisition of advanced technologies.

The financing of higher education raises some issues, though the amounts involved are not so great. Since university students are typically those who could achieve the most economically in any case and come from better-off families, an increase in state-supported university education is a redistribution from the poor to the better-off, on the average. In my judgement, a better system is to have the costs of a university education repaid by the student in subsequent years in an amount which depends on the former student's earnings. This could simply take the form of an additional small percentage increase in the income taxes of those whose university education was paid for by the state. Some such system is used in Australia today.

(d)   Child development: There is considerable evidence that cognitive abilities are greatly influenced by the family environment at very early ages, in particular the degree to which the child is stimulated. Unfortunately, (a) our knowledge is not yet great enough to permit much counselling or intervention, and (b) in any case, we do not know how to intervene successfully. Too much intervention undermines the family, and we do not have an adequate substitute.

2.3 *Capital*

The central role of capital formation in economic growth is unquestionable, though its exact importance is a matter of dispute. Capital formation is of course the same as saving out of current income. Saving is that part of income which is not consumed, capital formation is expenditure on capital goods; but total income in a closed economy is just the production of consumer and capital goods. Conventional economic analysis using standard tools would suggest that even a radical increase in the rate of savings will increase national income significantly only after a long period of time. A doubling of the savings rate might give rise to an increase of about 25% in annual income after a long period of time; and of course the higher savings rates mean lower consumption out of a given income, so that the gain in the welfare of the population is considerably less. Of course, extraordinary savings rates close to 50% such as are found in Singapore may indeed make a much larger difference. I understand that the savings ratio in Ireland in 1995 was 11.6% and that it fell about 2% in 1996.

Some would argue that the standard model understates the importance of capital formation. For example, it is held that new technologies appear in new capital goods, so that growing capital affords more opportunity for increasing efficiency. However, a comparison of the United States and Japan is illuminating in this respect. Despite much higher savings rates, Japan has not, in recent years, been increasing its productivity any more rapidly than the United Sates.

I have stressed the capital formed by domestic savings, since only such capital is actually owned by the citizens of the country. But foreign investment can also occur. Foreign investment is the counterpart of an excess of imports over exports (usually called an 'unfavourable balance of trade', but this is a misnomer; there is nothing unfavourable about an excess of imports over exports). Foreign investment may take the form of investment in public or private securities, which releases domestic funds for real investment, or it may take the form of direct investment (building of plants owned by foreign companies). It is usually small in magnitude compared with domestic investment. Its benefits are the additional output it creates (like domestic investment) and in particular an increased demand for certain kinds of labour and therefore higher wages (or reduced unemployment). Against this, of course, must be weighed the obligations to repay the investment with profit or interest.

The direct contribution of foreign investment to the economic growth of the citizens is apt to be fairly small. The real gains from foreign investment are improved competitivity and the transfer of knowledge to the country. In Ireland's case foreign investment has been especially significant in the high technology manufacturing sectors. In these, foreign industry accounts for about 90% of output. The 1,000 foreign-owned manufacturing and service firms account for around 70% of Ireland's industrial exports.

What can be produced by a labour force of given quantity and quality with a given body of capital goods and given natural resources is determined critically by the body of technical knowledge. Many, though not all, scholars would explain most of economic growth over time or differences among economic performance among countries at a given moment of time as attributable to variations in technological knowledge, knowledge how to produce goods.

Knowledge might be thought of as a kind of resource, an input into producing goods. But it is different in a fundamental way from other resources; it is not used up. If one firm or country has some knowledge, it can pass to another without the first firm or country losing it. This has profound effects on the incentives to create and use knowledge. In a world where many countries are engaged in science and technological development, a single country, especially a relatively small one such as Ireland, can argue that it can draw on scientific and technological developments elsewhere and need not invest much in research and development within its own borders. Many of my British colleagues feel that the United Kingdom has already gone down this path.

This argument is correct as far as it goes, but there is a countervailing point. Knowledge developed elsewhere is not made useful to Ireland automatically; it takes effort and understanding. It is necessary to have what development economists have called, 'absorptive capacity'. Among other factors is the presence of scientists and technologists who are up-to-date with new developments elsewhere. It is hard to have this domestic capacity to absorb foreign knowledge without a domestic ability to perform research and development at high levels.

As has been shown in a number of studies, foreign trade and especially foreign investment facilitate considerably the acquisition of new ideas from abroad. It is in the acquisition of knowledge from abroad that foreign trade and investment assume their greatest economic significance.

There is one note of warning about the international flow of ideas. There is a fallacious view that each country should strive to produce the technologically most advanced goods. This leads to policies that subsidise 'high-tech' industries. The countries of origin are likely to be ahead; in information industries, in particular, the advantage to the first mover is very considerable (though by no means absolute). In industries marked by progressive innovation, where continually newer varieties and qualities are appearing, the advantage to large countries with strong research infrastructures is too large to be overcome in general. Other countries have to stick to two principles: (1) take advantage of sources of comparative advantage, such as lower wages for equally qualified labour, to produce products that are not at the very edge of new quality but have become standardised commodities; (2) seek for individual niches which have not been exploited abroad. The latter policy requires the same basis as absorptive capacity, a strong basis of trained and experienced research personnel, and it also requires a competitive environment (see below).

3 Institutional Preconditions for Economic Growth

Comparisons of nations with very different rates of economic growth have made clear the great importance of the workings of political and economic institutions. Differences in the extent to which property rights are respected, the rule of law (permitting predictability in returns), and freedom from corruption lead to large differences in growth rates. However, these factors are undoubtedly not an issue in Ireland, however important they are in other parts of the world.

More relevant factors are the degree of competitiveness and the openness of the economy to the rest of the world. These are intimately connected. In a small country, it can easily happen that there are too few firms in an industry to permit adequate competition; foreign competition is needed. Competition is important partly to reduce markups and therefore increase consumer welfare but even more importantly to create a steady pressure for efficiency. The Latin American countries in particular had, until the last decade, a strong and sorry history of protecting domestic industries that they thought were ventures into new technology, only to create vast inefficiencies. It is also important to avoid creating monopolies or barriers to entry by offering subsidies or other privileges for the purpose of inducing foreign direct investments.

Flexibility in the labour market is also important to allow labour to flow from declining to rising industries. The price of this flexibility should not, however, fall on the workers; to avoid this, adequate unemployment compensation or other social safety nets are needed. Otherwise, there will be a political force to prevent declines in industry.

4   Macroeconomic Stability

I mention this for completeness, though the reminder may hardly be necessary in view of prevailing world opinion today. I refer to stability of both prices and aggregate demand. The details of achieving price stability are the subject of so much study that any further remarks are superfluous. Some attention must be paid to foreign exchange rates, particularly in the case of countries in which foreign trade is large relative to national income. If trade is mostly with countries that themselves have stable prices, then domestic stability will insure reasonably stable foreign exchange rates if they are flexible. Some economists argue that smaller countries are better off with fixed exchange rates against some large trading partner; I don't feel I know enough about this issue to comment.

Investment will stay away from the most productive channels if aggregate demand is highly variable; it will tend to flow towards safety and low returns. Therefore, stability of demand at a high level would be highly desirable. It may not be easily achievable by a small country. A large part of demand originates outside of the country, and attempts to stimulate demand by tax cuts or government expenditures will be partly diverted to demand for imports rather than home production. It would be desirable in the creation of the European-wide economy to have coordinated fiscal policy, but that does not seem to be on the current agenda. At a minimum, tax rates should not be raised during a recession in a misguided effort to balance the government budget on an annual basis.

This essay is too short for a summary. Briefly, the recommendations are to rely on the market system, domestic and global, and to facilitate it by removing obstacles to its working and by supplying the intellectual resources to improve the level of the labour force and to enable the local development of knowledge and the acquisition of knowledge from the rest of the world.

Poverty in Ireland and Anti-Poverty Strategy: A European Perspective

Anthony B. Atkinson*
Nuffield College, Oxford

I 3 ?
I 3 8

1 Introduction

In this essay, I am concerned with the problem of economic poverty in Ireland and anti-poverty strategy, viewed from a European perspective. In section 1, evidence about the extent and composition of poverty in Ireland is set alongside that for the European Union, and I ask how far we have seen the same trends over time in different countries. How does the poverty rate in Ireland compare with those in other Member States of the European Union? Did poverty in Europe rise with unemployment, or has the progressive development of social protection led to a reduction in poverty?

While poverty in European Union countries does not have the same claim on our attention as mass starvation in Africa, its existence and persistence represents, in my judgement, a major policy challenge for national governments and for the European Union. The Declaration at the 1995 Copenhagen Summit on Social Development committed countries to planning to:

> establish ... strategies and affordable time-bound goals and targets for the substantial reduction of overall poverty and the eradication of absolute poverty.

It was in response to this Summit that the Irish Government decided to develop the National Anti-Poverty Strategy. The Strategy Statement emphasised that:

> No society can view without deep concern the prospect of a significant minority of people becoming more removed from the incomes and life-style enjoyed by the majority .[1]

*I am grateful to Brian Nolan for his comments on a draft of this essay, without implicating him in anything that is said.

---

[1] National Anti-Poverty Strategy, 1997, p 4.

It went on to discuss the concrete actions which could be taken to tackle poverty. One important response must be through income maintenance policy, and section 3 of this paper examines its future role from a European standpoint. How far can social protection be provided solely by national governments? Does the European Union have an unavoidable role in guaranteeing a minimum level of social protection? If the European Union has a role, what form should be taken by the minimum social protection? Should it be a European version of the Supplementary Welfare Allowance? Or should it be a Basic Income?

Section 4 of the essay is motivated by the belief - shared by a number of the submissions to the National Anti-Poverty Strategy Committee - that anti-poverty policy should not be only a matter of income maintenance, important though this is. Poverty should be a priority concern in all aspects of economic policy. Economic and social issues are too often discussed in isolation, whereas they are deeply interconnected. This is illustrated by two examples of policy areas which affect the poor but where this impact is not typically taken into consideration: the tariff structure of utilities, and the criteria for macroeconomic policy.

2   Economic Poverty in Ireland and Europe

Poverty has many dimensions. Here attention is focused on economic poverty, that is poverty evaluated in terms of resources, whether income or expenditure. In so doing, I am not suggesting that this is the only facet of poverty which should be considered. However, I do believe that lack of economic resources is a major concern, both in itself and as a cause of powerlessness, insecurity, and social exclusion. People with low incomes or low levels of consumption are at greater risk of deprivation in other respects. At the same time, readers should recognise that the account given here needs to be supplemented with evidence about these other dimensions of poverty.

It should be noted that the evidence cited about economic poverty is limited to the household population, which means that important groups of the population, such as the homeless, travellers, and those living in institutions, are not covered. Since these groups are particularly vulnerable, the overall extent of poverty is almost certainly under-stated.

Knowledge about economic poverty has improved in recent years in all European Union countries, notably as a result of the increased availability of household surveys. These surveys provide information about the circumstances of individual households, which can be set against agreed poverty criteria to assess the extent and composition of poverty.

Such an improvement in knowledge has been seen in Ireland. The presentation by Ó Cinnéide (1972) to the Kilkenny Conference on Poverty had to piece together information from a variety of sources in order to arrive at an estimate of the extent of poverty. In 1976 the National Economic and Social Council commented on the limited information about the distribution of household incomes contained in official sources:

The data published to date ... have been extremely patchy.[2]

Since then the situation has been transformed. Information has become available from the 1973 and subsequent (1980, 1987 and 1994) Household Budget Surveys, the main purpose of which is to generate weights for the construction of the Consumer Price Index, but which also provides a basis for identifying households with low income or low expenditure. In 1987 there was, furthermore, the separate household survey carried out by the Economic and Social Research Institute (ESRI), one of whose major purposes was the measurement of poverty and deprivation (Callan et al, 1989, Nolan and Farrell, 1990, and Nolan and Callan, 1994). This in turn may be directly compared with the 1994 ESRI, Living in Ireland Survey (Callan et al, 1996), which forms the Irish component of the on-going European Community Household Panel.

There is now a wealth of data in Ireland on which we can draw in order to assess the distribution of income and the extent of economic poverty, by which I mean those people living in households which fall below a specified poverty line. The choice of such a poverty line is a complex issue (see, for example, in an Irish context, Callan and Nolan, 1991 and Nolan and Callan, 1994, Chapter 2). Here, given the European perspective, I simply follow the practice of Eurostat and

---

[2] Ó Cinnéide, 1980, p.137.

define the "EU" poverty line as 50% of the mean equivalent household income or total spending. "Equivalent" refers to the fact that the total for the household is divided by an "equivalence scale" to allow for differences in household size and composition. The scale used by Eurostat in a number of publications, referred to below as the "EU scale", is simplicity itself: 1 for a single person plus 0.7 for each additional person aged over 14 years and 0.5 for each person aged 14 or under. Reference is also made to a "modified EU" scale which replaces 0.7 by 0.5 and 0.5 by 0.3 in this formula, and thus gives less weight to larger households.

The use of 50% of average income (or spending) as the EU criterion is the concrete implementation of the decision by the Council of Ministers that the poor are:

> ... those whose resources (material, cultural and social) are so limited as to exclude them from the minimum acceptable way of life in the Member State in which they live.[3]

The exact percentage is essentially arbitrary, and one might argue that either 40% or 60% would be more appropriate, but it provides an indicator of the extent to which people fall behind the standard of living of the society of which they form part. Alternatively, it may be seen as an embodiment of the right of every citizen to a minimum level of resources, where the choice of 50% has the merit of being a transparent and easily communicated definition.

In order to put the Irish situation in perspective, I begin with the European statistics on economic poverty produced on behalf of Eurostat by Hagenaars et al (1994). It is very difficult to put such statistics on a comparable basis, but the Eurostat study has made major progress in this direction. It assembled data from the same kind of source: household budget surveys, in the Irish case the Household Budget Survey for 1987. It had access to the micro-data so that variables could be constructed on the same basis and the same definitions applied. At the same time, differences remain. Budget surveys differ across countries in the extent to which they fully record income and spending: the income data in some countries are considerably more incomplete than in others. Standardisation on a common definition may have different implications depending on the choice: for example, using one particular equivalence scale to adjust for differences in household size, rather than another, may affect the comparison of two countries with different household compositions.

---

[3]Council Decision, 19 December 1984.

These qualifications should be borne in mind when viewing the estimates shown in Figure 1 for the European Community (as it was then), excluding Luxembourg, in the late 1980s. The diagram shows the percentage of households below the EU poverty line, applying the modified EU equivalence scale, and using both total spending and total income as yardsticks. There are some major discrepancies (for example, Denmark and Italy), but the estimates on the two bases are broadly similar: for example, 15.8% of households in Ireland are below the poverty line on a spending basis and 13.8% on an income basis. The countries are ranked from left to right in order of poverty as measured on a spending basis. Ireland is broadly in the middle, with the countries of Northern Europe tending to have lower poverty rates and those of Southern Europe tending to have higher poverty.

Figure 1 Poverty in EU Countries - Late 1980s
Modified EU Equivalence Scale

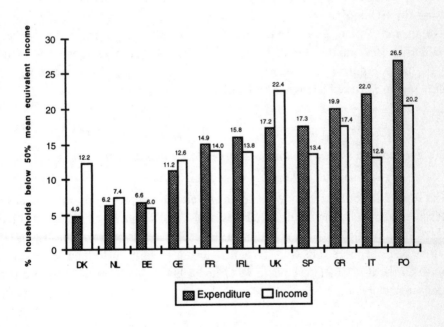

Source: Vos and Zaidi, 1995, Tables 3.1 and 3.2.

13

The composition of the poverty population is illustrated in Figures 2a-2d for four European countries (Ireland, France, Italy and the UK), where poor households are classified according to the socio-economic category of the head of household. This shows some interesting country differences. Unemployment of the household head stands out in Ireland, accounting for nearly a third. In the other three countries, the retired are the largest group. Farmers and agricultural workers are more important in Ireland, France and Italy than the UK. Home-makers are a larger proportion in Ireland than in France and Italy. Among the factors explaining these differences are differences in the national economies, in demographic and household structure, and in national social protection systems. Such differences are an important consideration when we come to consider anti-poverty policies from a European perspective.

The position in Ireland in 1987 has been examined in greater detail by the ESRI using their household survey for that year which contains detailed information about incomes (but not total spending). The findings for the overall extent of poverty are similar: they find that 17.6% of households are below the poverty line using the EU equivalence scale (Callan et al, 1996, Table 4.9). They also find (Nolan and Callan, 1992) that poverty in Ireland was substantially higher in Ireland in 1987 than in Great Britain in 1985. This finding appears to conflict with that in Figure 1, but poverty was rising rapidly in the UK at that time while showing less marked change in Ireland, as is shown in the next section.

2.2 Trend in Poverty in Ireland and Other European Countries

The sensitivity of the measured level of poverty to the precise definitions utilised has been shown by the careful analyses of the ESRI data (for example, Callan et al, 1989 and 1996, Nolan and Callan, 1994). The trends over time in Ireland turn out to be even more sensitive. Whether or not poverty in Ireland has increased between the two ESRI surveys in 1987 and 1994 depends on the definitions and measures adopted.

14

Figures 2a - 2d: Composition of Poor

Figure 2a: - Ireland

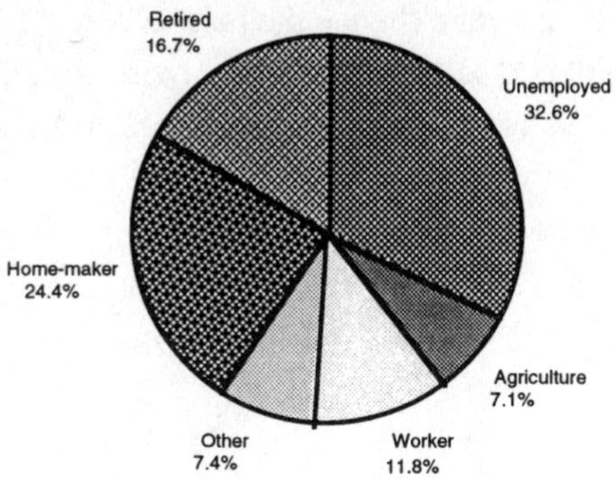

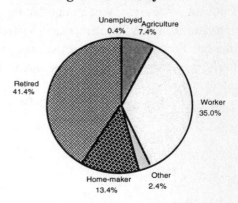

Figure 2c: - Italy

Figure 2b: - France

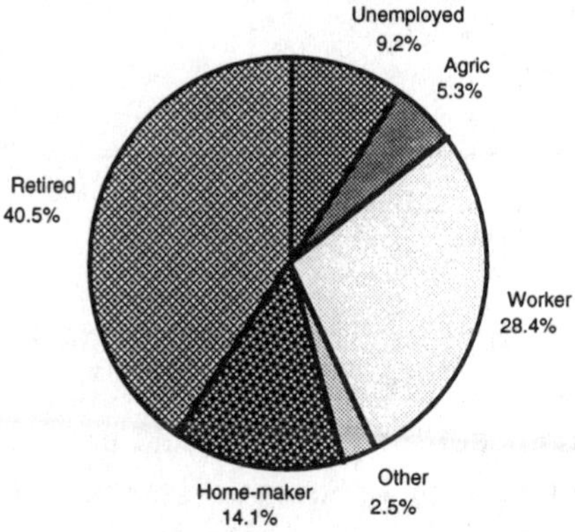

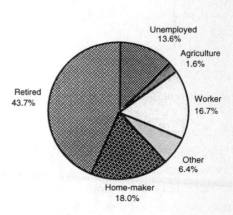

Figure 2d: - UK

Note: Expenditure basis: % households below 50% mean modified EU equivalence scale

Source: Vos and Zaidi, 1995, Tables A3.1, A3.3, A3.7 and A3.8.

The household survey carried out by ESRI for 1994 was designed to allow estimates to be made comparable with those for 1987. A selection of findings are shown in Figures 3a-3c. A Pessimist would be impressed by the set of estimates in Figure 3a labelled SWA. These show a rise in poverty (in each case I have normalised so that 1987 = 100); in fact poverty rose from 16.3% to 18.5%. An Optimist however may point out that this depends on using the equivalence scale approximating the Supplementary Welfare Allowance (hence the label SWA). If, like true Europeans, we adopt the EU equivalence scale, which gives more weight to children, then poverty appears to have fallen as shown by the line labelled EU.

Figure 3a: Change in Poverty in Ireland (1987=100)

Different Equivalence Scales

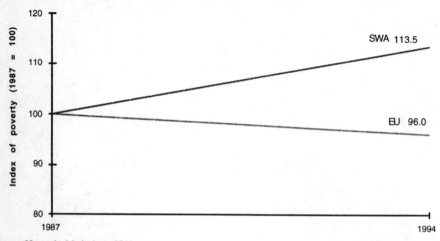

Note: Households below 50% mean

The Pessimist now returns to the attack with Figure 3b. Here he accepts the EU scale, but takes the Optimist to task for counting households. After all, in a democratic society surely each person should count for 1? We should not give the same weight to a single person as to a couple with 4 children. This takes us from the line labelled "Households" to that labelled "Persons". Poverty has increased. However, the Optimist, while agreeing that the number of people in poverty has risen, goes on to argue that we should be concerned not just with counting the number of poor people but with how far they fall below the poverty line. If a family is £1 a month below the poverty line, this is less serious than if they are £50 below. This points to measuring the *poverty gap*, rather than the number of persons, and the poverty gap has fallen - see Figure 3c. Serious poverty is less than it was.

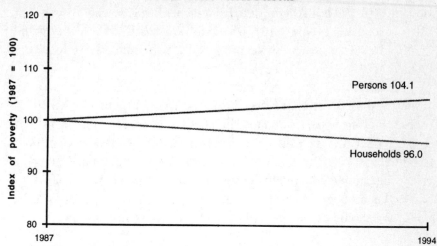

Figure 3b: Change in Poverty in Ireland (1987=100)

Households versus Persons

Note : Below 50% mean with EU scale

Figure 3c: Change in Poverty in Ireland (1987=100)

Headcount versus Poverty Gap

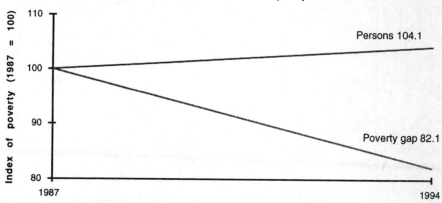

Note: Below 50% mean with EU scale

Source: Callan et al, 1996, Tables 4.9 and 4.10.

This dialogue shows that there is no simple answer. At the same time, one feature is clear: the changes are relatively modest. Neither the increase, if there has been one, nor any decrease, is dramatic. The same is true over the longer period 1973 to 1994, linking results from the earlier Household Budget Surveys (Callan et al, 1996, Table 4.13), which show a fall in the poverty count from 18.9% to 16.9% on a household basis and a rise from 18.6% to 22.9% on a persons basis.

The person-based estimates are those shown in Figure 4a, which allow a comparison of the *trends* with those in other EU countries. The word "trends" is italicised, since the data do not allow comparisons of the *level* of poverty in different countries. The estimates in Figure 4a for Belgium and France are not directly comparable with the Irish estimates. (For example, the figures for France are based on a poverty line of 50% of the *median*, not the mean as in the Irish figures. We should expect them to be lower on this account.)

Figure 4a: Trends in Poverty I

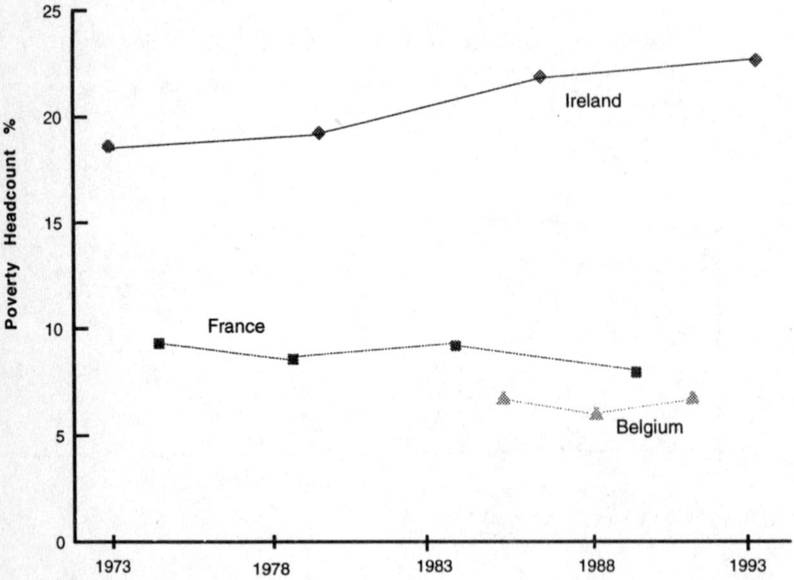

18

There is in fact a variety of patterns in different EU countries. The figures for France and Belgium were relatively stable over this period. In Scandinavia, shown in Figure 4b, poverty in Denmark was relatively stable, that in Finland showed a quite noticeable decline, and that in Sweden increased, from a low base. Increases are also shown in Figure 4c. In West Germany, as in Sweden, there was a definite upward trend over the 1980s and the first half of the 1990s. In Italy, poverty rose from 1980 to 1988, but then fell back (it should be noted that these estimates are on an expenditure basis, and that income data show a less sharp rise - see Cannari and Franco, 1997). Finally, the United Kingdom stands out for its sharp rise in poverty in the second part of the 1980s which has not been reversed. The magnitude of the rise should be stressed: if poverty in the UK were initially well below that in Ireland, then it may well have risen to a similar level by the 1990s.

Figure 4b: Trends in Poverty II

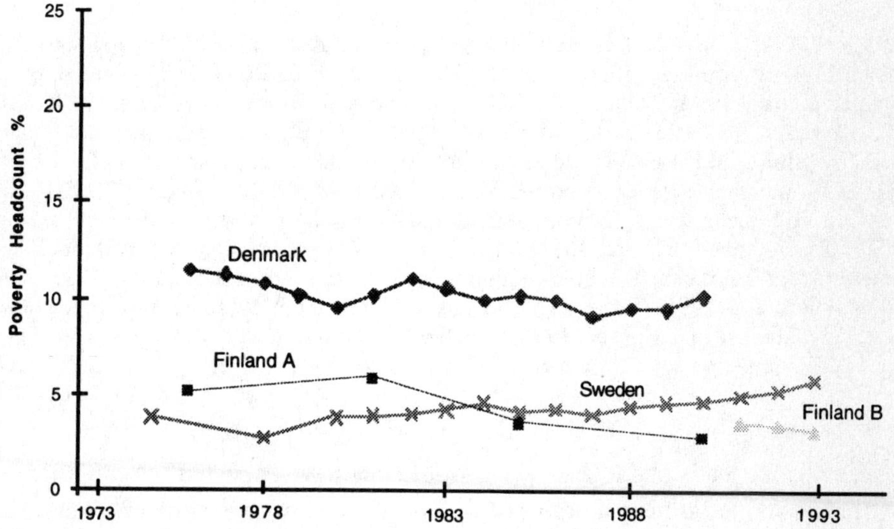

Figure 4c: Trends in Poverty III

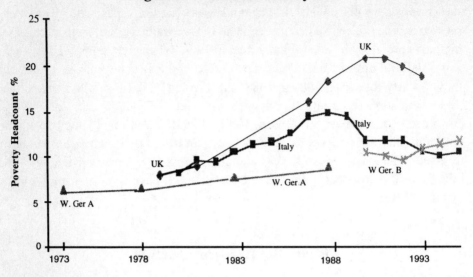

Sources (Figures 4a-4c): Ireland: Callan et al, 1996, Table 4.13, EU scale, persons, 50% mean; France:Synthèses, 1995, page 56, EU scale, households, 50% median; Belgium: Cantillon et al, 1994, Tableau 10, EU scale, persons, 50% mean; Denmark: Nordisk Ministerråd, 1996, Figur 1, page 35, persons aged 18-75, EU scale, 50% median; Finland: Nordisk Ministerråd, 1996, Tabell 1, page 67, equivalence scale square root of household size, 50% median; Sweden: Nordisk Ministerråd, 1996, Figur 2, page 152, EU scale, persons, 50% mean; Italy: Commissione di indagine sulla poverta e sull'emarginazione, 1996, Tav. 1, page 15, and 1996a, Tav.1, page 7, Commissione equivalence scale, households, 50% mean; United Kingdom: Department of Social Security, 1992, 1993, 1994, 1995, and 1996, Table F1, DSS equivalence scale, persons, 50% mean; West Germany: Becker and Hauser, 1996, Tabelle 3 in first lecture and Tabelle 3 in second lecture, EU scale, persons, 50% mean.

This evidence leads one to ask - what would one have expected? Again there are Optimists and Pessimists in terms of the way they view this evidence. Pessimists would have expected a general improvement, as social transfers became more effective, as the elderly became more able to save, as family size became smaller, and more women entered the paid labour force. The Pessimist might have expected a pattern like that of Finland and hence be disappointed that few countries have shared this path.

20

Optimists, however, would take comfort in the European record. After all, they would argue, we would have expected the massive rise in European unemployment to have led to large increases in poverty. The UK picture is what we expected, and we should be pleased that most countries avoided such a shocking rise in poverty. They were able to do so because their systems of social protection replace a substantial fraction of lost income. The record is one of success for the European Welfare State.

Whichever way one interprets the evidence, poverty remains a major European problem. Reforms to social policy in order to address this problem are the subject to which I turn in section 3. Before that, I consider the relation between income and other indicators of deprivation.

2.3 *Income Poverty and Exclusion from Consumption*

One interesting feature of the ESRI 1987 and 1994 household surveys is that respondents were asked, in addition to income questions, about their life-style with the intention of obtaining direct measures of deprivation. As noted by Callan et al:

> ... it is valuable to complement income measures with direct indicators of the extent and nature of deprivation and exclusion being experienced by households. [4]

The life-style questions covered twenty indicators, where respondents were asked whether they have the item in question, and whether they are doing without it because of lack of money. They drew on the work of Townsend (1979) and Mack and Lansley (1985) in the United Kingdom. Where an item is not possessed, and this is stated to be because it could not be afforded, then it is said to be "enforced lack". They also make use of supplementary information (about meals, heating, evenings out, and arrears).

---

[4] Callan et al, 1994, p 43.

This approach may be seen as constructing a direct measure of exclusion from consumption, and it is interesting to ask how far this overlaps with low income. Callan et al (1996, Table 6.7) concentrate on enforced "basic deprivation", based on food (for instance, "going without a substantial meal"), going without heating, clothing, and debt problems. Figure 5 shows the degree of overlap between those households with low income (measured on a household basis and using the SWA equivalence scale) and those with enforced basic deprivation. If there were no relation, then we would have the dashed line in Figure 5, labelled "Independent". In fact those with low income are much more likely to suffer basic deprivation than those above the income cut-off. At the same time, the overlap is not complete (and the composition of the two populations is different).

Figure 5 Overlap between Income, Poverty and Enforced Basic Deprivation in Ireland 1994

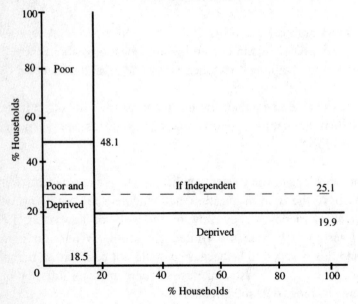

Source: Callan et al, 1996, calculated from Tables 4.7, 6.6 and 6.7.

What do we make of the limited overlap? Our Optimist may argue that poverty and deprivation are measured with error, so that we should only really look at those households who show up on both indicators. Those with low income but no basic deprivation are, on this argument, probably only passing through a temporary phase, or there may be a simple explanation like recording error. Those who do not meet the consumption criteria, even though they are above the income cut-off, may, on this argument, be choosing a different life-style, or have given a misleading answer. This is an optimistic view, since the overlap is 8.9% of households, which makes the problem seem much more manageable.

The Pessimist, however, may argue that there are really two different, legitimate sources of concern: one is with living standards, captured by the deprivation index, the other is with the right to a minimum level of resources, measured here by current income. (This aspect is discussed by Callan et al, 1994, p 62.) On this argument, we *are* concerned about people who show up on one but not both of the criteria. The right to a minimum is independent of how the person exercises consumption choices, but at the same time we are worried if old people have inadequate heating irrespective of their income levels. This is a pessimistic position in that the combination of the two groups is close to a third of total households.

2.4 *Concluding Comment*

Consideration of the empirical evidence about poverty is important both because it allows us to judge the quantitative importance of the substantive issue and because it forces us to think more carefully about the objectives of policy. Why exactly are we concerned about poverty and how do we wish to measure it?

3   Anti-Poverty Strategy: Towards a European Social Minimum?

Policy to tackle poverty is at heart a national matter. In Ireland, it has been taken as a major issue by successive governments. In the 1980s the Commission on Social Welfare (1986) carried out an extensive review of social protection, making a series of significant recommendations, which have influenced subsequent policy with regard to benefit levels and structure. A 1986 Act established the Combat Poverty Agency as a catalyst for change. There has been an active debate about radical reforms such as the introduction of a basic income (Expert Working Group on the Integration of the Tax and Social Welfare Systems, 1996, and Clark and Healy, 1997). As noted at the outset of this essay, in response to the Declaration at the United Nations World Summit in Copenhagen, the Irish Government set up an Interdepartmental Policy Committee charged with drawing up a National Anti-Poverty Strategy, which in 1997 produced the Strategy Statement.

Here, I do not attempt to comment on the details of Irish national policy. Instead I consider the function and form of Europe-wide anti-poverty policy. The first question is, of course, whether there is any legitimate role for action at the European level to secure a minimum income.

3.1 Europe-Wide versus National Social Policy

In the early days of the European Community, social policy received relatively little attention, and the Community's organs were provided with very limited powers in the social field. Social policy was a means towards achieving other objectives, such as removing barriers to labour mobility and ensuring that differences in the costs of social protection did not prevent competition in the supply of goods. In the 1970s the social dimension of the Community began to play a more important role. The Commission produced a Social Action Programme, accepted by the Council in 1974, which recognised that the Community had an independent role to play in the formation of social policy and that it should implement, in co-operation with Member States, specific measures to combat poverty. This led in July 1975 to the first European Action Programme covering the period 1975-1980. In December 1981, the Commission made an evaluation report, containing a widely publicised estimate of the number of poor people in the Community. Despite the concern generated by these figures, it took several years to agree the Second Action Programme for the period 1985-1989 (evaluated in Commission of the European Communities, 1989). This was followed by a third programme stressing social exclusion and marginalisation, but the proposed subsequent Fourth Poverty programme was vetoed by Britain and Germany in 1995.

At the same time, the social dimension was receiving more attention generally in the Community. In 1989 the Commission put forward a draft of the Community Charter of Fundamental Social Rights and this was adopted in modified form at the Strasbourg European Council in December 1989 by 11 of the 12 Member States. The opposition of the United Kingdom at the Maastricht European Council led to the Social Chapter as such being excluded from the final Treaty on European Union, but there was an attached Social Protocol. Whether or not there can be action at the European level depends on how far social protection is deemed to be within the competence of the European Union. This brings us to the principle of subsidiarity. Article 3b of the Treaty on European Union states that:

> ... the Community shall take action, in accordance with the principle of subsidiarity, only if and insofar as the objectives of the proposed action cannot be sufficiently achieved by the member states and can therefore, by reason of the scale or effects of the proposed action, be better achieved by the Community.

It should be noted that the Article refers explicitly to *the objectives of the proposed action*. In other words, it does not leave the lower level government free to determine the *objectives* of redistributive policy. If the European Union as a whole is concerned to abolish poverty, then the implication is that the European Union should act to support the social protection activities of Member States and to fill the gaps which remain at the national level. The Union should 'supplement' national activity when the demands of justice exceed their capacities.

The capacities of Member States to combat poverty are indeed under threat. Sinn has argued forcefully that fiscal competition means that:

> ... the poor will lose because governments will no longer be able to maintain their current scales of redistribution. ... it will be difficult for a single country to extract the required funds from the rich. On the other hand, net benefits being given to the poor in one jurisdiction will attract poor people from everywhere and so make this policy unsustainable. The New York city effect will be the death of Europe's welfare states if the unmitigated competition of tax systems is allowed.[5]

---

[5] Sinn, 1990, pp. 501-502.

Such a contention suggests that the national governments may indeed be in need of Union assistance in ensuring adequate social protection. National governments will be under pressure to reduce transfers to the poor.

Now it may be objected that Sinn's argument relies on the impact of migration of labour, and there are good reasons to doubt whether this will be of sufficient quantitative importance, at least in the foreseeable future. The evidence from the US about 'welfare migration' between states with different levels of benefits (for example, Peterson and Rom, 1990) suggests that there is a significant effect, but that its quantitative magnitude is rather small. If we turn to the effect on contributors, rather than beneficiaries, then the evidence for the European Union to date does not suggest that substantial migration has been induced by the significant differences which exist between Member States in net of tax wage rates. Ermisch after examining the evidence for different countries noted:

> ... the failure of the pattern or volume of migration among EC countries to change much after the formation of the EC[6].

The mechanism may however not be actual migration, but *potential*, or threatened, movement of labour or investment. Workers who perceive that taxes are lower in other Member States may not migrate but may seek to exercise political power to achieve lower taxes at home. Businesses who fear that other countries have a cost advantage may bring pressure to bear on politicians, claiming that jobs will be lost unless taxes and social charges are reduced. Comparisons of tax rates with those in other member countries feature prominently in national election campaigns. These political economy considerations are an important restriction on the freedom of national governments to carry out social protection, and I believe that a Europe-wide anti-poverty policy can be justified on these grounds.

3.2 *Form of the European Minimum*

If a social dimension to the Union is to develop alongside the Internal Market and the Monetary Union, then what form should the European minimum take? The Social Charter refers to people with "no means of subsistence" being able to "receive sufficient resources and social assistance in keeping with their particular

---

[6] Ermisch, 1991, p.101.

situation." This appears to envisage a form of income-tested social assistance. This would be in line with the recent introduction of generalised social assistance schemes in a number of Member States, such as the Revenu Minimum d'Insertion in France, and the experiments with a minimum income in Portugal.

The UK has, however, extensive experience of means-tested programmes, and this leads me to doubt whether this is the appropriate route for Europe to follow. I say this for four reasons:

(a) means-tested programmes are highly complex and difficult to harmonise: for example, problems arise with the definition of resources taken into account, the period over which they are measured, and the degree to which other transfers are taken into account,

(b) means-tested benefits depend on a concept of liability to maintain, which differs considerably across Member States (such as the liability in Germany of relatives not resident in the household), and which goes against the widespread trend towards the individualisation of benefit and tax systems,

(c) withdrawal of assistance leads to high marginal tax rates on additional earnings, or on the income which people have saved for old age, and the potential disincentives may affect all members of the family unit, leading to withdrawal of partners or adult children from the labour force,

(d) the status of assistance as a 'residual' benefit risks recipients feeling excluded or stigmatised, and in some countries there is evidence that this leads to incomplete take-up of the benefit; while this may be interpreted positively, as evidence of people securing their independence, it means that there are people living below the specified minimum.

For these reasons, I do not consider means-testing the way forward. In my view, we need to combine elements of 'Old' in the form of social insurance, which is the backbone of the social transfer system in all European countries, and 'New' in the form of a Participation Income, which is a conditional citizen's income.

Social insurance, which provides benefits to people as individuals without tests of means, enjoys considerable public support, including the confidence of the social partners. Diversity can be accommodated, with appropriate provision for those working in more than one country. Social insurance is less subject to the downward pressures of fiscal competition, since social insurance furnishes a transparent link between contributions and benefits. What one has to look at is the *net benefit* from the social insurance scheme, and this may well make countries with high levels of social protection attractive to prospective workers.

There are, at the same time, limitations to social insurance. There are significant gaps in coverage. Social insurance, which had its origins in the modern employment relationship, does not always recognise the needs of those outside the formal economy, such as people taking care of dependant relatives. It may exclude those who have not had labour market attachment, such as those disabled from birth, or young people entering the labour market for the first time, or married women returning to work when their children have ceased to be dependant. There may be difficulties in providing for part-time employees and for the more flexible working arrangements that are likely to characterise the next century. It cannot readily allow for people opting out of the formal employment status for significant periods of their lives, pursuing some alternative life-style.

The limitations of social insurance are one reason why the idea of a basic income, or citizen's income, has been put forward as an alternative. In its pure form, the basic income would replace all existing social insurance and assistance benefits by a single payment, paid on an individual basis, without any test of means, and paid unconditionally. The benefit would also replace all income tax allowances, and in this sense there would be an integration of taxation and social security, although the tax would be collected in a separate operation. In the simplest form of the scheme, there would be a single tax rate on all income, but there could be a differentiated rate structure.

In my view, it is, however, a mistake to see basic income as an *alternative* to social insurance. It is more productive to see basic income as complementary. For this reason, I am much more persuaded by the approach to basic income adopted in the United Kingdom by Parker (1989). She outlines a scheme which would replace tax allowances, although retaining an earned income disregard, but would keep the existing structure of social insurance benefits. While she regards this as the first phase of a move to a basic income, I see this partnership between social insurance and basic income not just as a transitional compromise but as an alternative conception of the basic income.

But this is not enough to ensure political support. It is noteworthy that, despite the attention which basic income has been given, and despite finding supporters in a range of political parties, the scheme has not got close to being introduced. If one asks why, then in my judgement a major reason for opposition to basic income lies in its lack of conditionality. There are concerns that it will lead to dependency, or state-induced social exclusion. I believe therefore that, in order to secure political support, it may be necessary for the proponents of basic income to compromise - not on the principle of getting rid of the means test, nor on the principle of independence, but on the unconditional payment.

This has led me to propose a basic income conditional on *participation* (Atkinson, 1995, Chapter 15). The way in which this participation requirement would be defined requires detailed consideration, but qualifying conditions would include (a) work as an employee or self-employed, (b) absence from work on grounds of sickness, injury, or disability, (c) being unemployed but available for work, (d) reaching pension age, (e) engaging in approved forms of education or training, and (f) caring for young, elderly or disabled dependants. As the last examples make clear, the condition is not *paid* work; it is a wider definition of social contribution. The determination of these conditions would undoubtedly involve problems, problems which would not arise with the unconditional basic income. And these problems would mean that there were people who failed to secure the basic income. There would also be behavioural responses, as people adjusted their actions in order to qualify. On the other hand, these adjustments would be in the direction of social inclusion: for example, an unemployed person who undertook part-time work would be *qualifying* rather than the reverse.

A Participation Income provides, in my view, a better basis for establishing a European minimum, offering the possibility of establishing minimum standards for nationally-provided benefits. The first step should be the setting of a minimum basic income for children, but the next stage should be the identification of conditions under which a basic income would be guaranteed to adults (where the precise form of delivery could vary from country to country). I believe that such a Participation Income offers a realistic way of persuading European governments that there is a better route forward than the dead end of means tested assistance.

4   Giving Priority to Poverty in Economic Policy

Successful anti-poverty policy requires not just the conventional armoury of weapons against poverty - such as improved social transfers - but also that poverty be given priority in all areas of economic policy. The objective of combating poverty should be incorporated within all areas of government policy. A number of submissions to the Irish Inter-departmental Policy Committee proposed that:

... all public bodies should be required to 'poverty proof' all policies and actions.[7]

In this section, I give two examples of areas of economic policy where poverty does not typically receive attention, but where the decisions of industrial policy-makers or macroeconomic policy-makers may have profound consequences for the poor in Europe.

4.1 Pricing Policy, Exclusion of Consumers and Privatisation

The first example goes back to exclusion in terms of life-styles: whether people are able to participate in everyday consumption activities, like heating their house or having a telephone (which nowadays may be an essential aid to securing employment). Whether they can do so is in part a matter of income, but there is also a second side to the market, which is the terms of which goods and services are supplied. In particular, the pricing policies of suppliers may exacerbate the position of the poor - a fact that is well known to those who provide welfare advice, but which does not usually feature in economic policy debate.

---

[7] Summary of Submissions on the National Anti-Poverty Strategy, 1995, p. 28.

This means that, in seeking to understand the causes of exclusion, we need to look at the ways in which suppliers determine their pricing schedules. In particular, how do they balance the cost per unit (per kilowatt or per call) against the fixed charge which they make to each household? (Of course, actual tariffs are more complicated.) If they are aiming to maximise profits, then there is no reason why they should set the fixed charge at a level low enough that it can be afforded by the poorest households. If there is not a sufficient number of people with low incomes to offset the gain from charging an extra £1 to all other consumers, then some people will be excluded from the market by the pricing structure. (It should be noted that this argument has nothing to do with the poor being regarded as less satisfactory credit risks; it would be true even if everyone pre-paid.) From this, we can see that the level of the fixed charge depends on the distribution of income in the society as a whole. As others get richer, leaving the poor behind, so too it will become more likely that the poor are excluded, since the fixed charge will rise. Put differently, the minimum income needed to participate in a consumption activity may have to rise as the general level of incomes rises.

This view of social exclusion points to ways in which the impact on the poor needs to be taken into account in designing economic policy. Poverty may well be a relevant consideration, for example, when considering competition policy: whether or not the government allows mergers or take-overs, and the steps taken to encourage competition in product markets. If consumers are excluded by the current pricing structure, then a new entrant may tap the excluded section of the market by setting a lower fixed charge, which would be of benefit in terms of anti-poverty policy. Or the threat of new entry may prevent existing suppliers from pricing the poor out of the market. At the same time, we should note that there is no guarantee that free entry would have this effect: the outcome depends on the strategic interaction. All that is being argued here is that the non-exclusion of poor consumers should be a criterion when judging competition policy.

These considerations are important when it comes to privatisation of previously public utilities. Whereas it would be open to the government to instruct *public* enterprises to choose a tariff structure such that, for example, households living on social assistance can afford electricity, privatisation requires that some mechanism be put in place to avoid exclusion of low income customers, since this may well be profitable for the new management. Where the industry is regulated, then an access condition can be imposed by the regulators. In the case of telephones in the United States,

> "Universal Access" has been a historical commitment of the telecommunications industry and its regulators.[8]

In the UK analysis of privatisation, little reference has been made to this access question. It is a further illustration of the need to bring consideration of poverty into broader economic policy.

4.2 *Macroeconomic Criteria and the Case for a Poverty Criterion*

I turn now to a second area where poverty should be given greater priority: in the debate about macroeconomic policy. One of the causes of the rise in poverty in the UK over the 1980s was the scaling-back of social security benefits. The level of the basic retirement pension has fallen relative to average net incomes, because it has been indexed to prices rather than earnings at a time when real earnings have increased significantly. The coverage of benefits has been reduced through the tightening of contribution and other conditions. There have been major cuts in unemployment insurance, which has now been replaced by the Job Seekers Allowance. These measures were taken by the Conservative Government in part because they believed that they would increase labour market flexibility, but a major consideration has been to reduce public spending. This in turn originated partly in ideological beliefs but also reflected the demands of macroeconomic policy-making. In other European countries, pressures for cutting spending on social transfers have arisen in the 1990s as a result of seeking to meet the Maastricht criteria on public deficit and debt levels.

---

[8] Gillis et al, 1986, p 35.

In the macroeconomic debate, poverty typically does not feature. If one reads macroeconomic textbooks, one gets the impression that distributional issues are irrelevant, or that any distributional consequences can be dealt with appropriate - unspecified - social policy. But the cost of dealing with the social costs of macro-policy is one of the sources of the fiscal problems with which governments are now seeking to grapple.

We need to ensure that the impact on the poor is borne fully in mind in the discussion of macro-policy. It should be a priority of the Department of Finance as well as the Ministry of Social Welfare. How can this be achieved?

In my view, we can learn from the experience with anti-inflation policy. In October 1992, after the pound had left the Exchange Rate Mechanism, the United Kingdom government launched a new macroeconomic strategy, at the heart of which was a formal target for the rate of inflation. Although low inflation had been long an avowed objective, there had not previously been an explicit quantitative performance standard. The government now announced its intention to keep inflation within a range of 1 to 4 percent. These were fine words, and the problem was to make them credible. Credibility was sought by increasing the role of the Bank of England, including the innovation of introducing a quarterly *Inflation Report* (see King, 1994), providing statistical evidence about inflation and its prospects, together with a commentary.

The argument which I have made in the United Kingdom (Atkinson, 1996) is that those concerned with the abolition of poverty can draw on the parallel with inflation policy. Reducing poverty should become an explicit object of policy. There should be a poverty criterion, which governments accept as a commitment, and there should be an official *Poverty Report* assessing how far the target has been reached. In a European context, it would mean adding poverty to the convergence criteria, with a European body charged with monitoring progress. There are already official Eurostat figures on poverty, and these are much to be welcomed, but the simple publication of statistics is not enough. We require, as it is put in the Irish Anti-Poverty Strategy Statement:

> ... the adoption of clear overall objectives, targets and policy actions ... designed to demonstrate to everyone the ongoing process.[9]

---

[9] 1997, p. 4.

The reduction of poverty has to be an official ambition, just like the reduction of inflation. The figures in the *Poverty Report* have to be seen as indicating how far we are from achieving our goal.

What form would the poverty objective take? In Europe we have seen the dangers of fixed targets, in the Maastricht criteria. It does not seem reasonable to see the elimination of poverty as a fixed target. Rather, it is a criterion by which performance is judged, alongside the inflation, deficit and other macroeconomic figures. The Pessimist may question whether there could be agreement on the precise definition of the poverty criterion. As we have seen in section 2, whether or not poverty has increased in Ireland depends sensitively on the choice of indicator. The Optimist, on the other hand, will draw the lesson that we need to think more deeply about the nature of social objectives, and that this process can only be beneficial to rational design of policy.

5 Conclusions

Economic poverty appears, from the available evidence, to be a significant problem, touching at least 1 in 10 of Irish households. Poverty in Ireland is less than in some Member States of the European Union, but is above that in Northern Europe. The adoption of the Irish Anti-Poverty Strategy is therefore of great importance.

Anti-poverty policy is essentially a national responsibility, but the potential problems of fiscal competition mean that national governments may need European Union assistance in ensuring adequate social protection. The way forward for an effective social minimum in Europe is, in my judgement, not via means-tested benefits but through a partnership between established social insurance and a new Participation Income.

Poverty needs to feature in all aspects of economic policy-making, as illustrated here by the examples of competition policy and macroeconomic policy. The exclusion of consideration of the poor from the economic debate is just another manifestation of their risk of exclusion from society as a whole.

References

Atkinson, A. B., 1995, *Incomes and the Welfare State*, Cambridge University Press, Cambridge.

Atkinson, A. B., 1996, "Promise and Performance: Why We Need an Official Poverty Report", in P. Barker, editor, *Living as Equals*, Oxford University Press, Oxford.

Becker, I. and R. Hauser, 1996, "Einkommensverteilung und Armut in Deutschland von 1962 bis 1995", Arbeitspapier Nr. 7, Johann Wolfgang Goethe-Universität, Frankfurt am Main.

Callan, T. and B. Nolan, 1991, "Concepts of poverty and the poverty line: a critical survey of approaches to measuring poverty", *Journal of Economic Surveys*, 5, pp.243-262.

Callan, T., B. Nolan, and C. T. Whelan, 1994, "Income, Deprivation, and Exclusion" in B. Nolan and T. Callan, 1994, editors, *Poverty and Policy in Ireland*, Gill and Macmillan, Dublin.

Callan, T., B. Nolan, and B. J. Whelan, D. F. Hannan, with S. Creighton, 1989, *Poverty, Income and Welfare in Ireland*, Paper No. 146, ESRI, Dublin.

Callan, T., B. Nolan, and C. T. Whelan, 1993, "Resources, Deprivation and the Measurement of Poverty", *Journal of Social Policy*, 22, pp.141-172.

Callan, T., B. Nolan, B. J. Whelan, C. T. Whelan and J. Williams, 1996, *Poverty in the 1990s*, Oak Tree Press, Dublin.

Cannari, L. and D. Franco, 1997, "La povertà tra i minorenni in Italia: dimensioni, caratteristiche, politiche", *Temi di discussione*, Numero 294, Banca D'Italia, Rome.

Cantillon, B., I. Marx, D. Proost and R. Van Dam, 1994, *Indicateurs Sociaux: 1985 - 1992*, Centrum voor Sociaal Beleid, University of Antwerp.

Commission of the European Communities, 1989, *Interim Report on a Specific Community Action Programme to Combat Poverty*, European Commission, Brussels.

Commission on Social Welfare, 1986, *Report*, Stationery Office, Dublin.

Commissione di indagine sulla povertà e sull'emarginazione, 1996, *La Povertà in Italia 1980-1994*, Presidenza del Consiglio dei Ministri, Rome.

Commissione di indagine sulla povertà e sull'emarginazione, 1996a, *La Povertà in Italia 1995*, Presidenza del Consiglio dei Ministri, Rome.

Clark, C. M. A. and J. Healy, 1997, *Pathways to a Basic Income*, CORI, Dublin.

Department of Social Security, 1992, *Households Below Average Income: A Statistical Analysis 1979-1988/89*, HMSO, London.

Department of Social Security, 1993, *Households Below Average Income: A Statistical Analysis 1979-1990/91*, HMSO, London.

Department of Social Security, 1994, *Households Below Average Income: A Statistical Analysis 1979-1991/92*, HMSO, London.

Department of Social Security, 1995, *Households Below Average Income: A Statistical Analysis 1979-1992/93*, HMSO, London.

Department of Social Security, 1996, *Households Below Average Income: A Statistical Analysis 1979-1993/94*, HMSO, London.

Ermisch, J., 1991, "European integration and external constraints on social policy: is a Social Charter necessary?", *National Institute Economic Review*, May, pp.93-108.

Expert Working Group on the Integration of the Tax and Social Welfare Systems, 1996, *Integrating Tax and Social Welfare*, Stationery Office, Dublin.

Gillis, M., G. Jenkins and J. Leitzel, 1986, "Financing universal access in the telephone network", *National Tax Journal*, 39, pp.35-48.

Hagenaars, A., K. De Vos and A. Zaidi, 1994, *Poverty Statistics in the late 1980s*, Eurostat, Luxembourg.

King, M. A., 1994, "Monetary Policy", *Fiscal Studies*, 15, pp.109-128.

Mack, J. and S. Lansley, 1985, *Poor Britain*, Allen and Unwin, London.

National Anti-Poverty Strategy, 1997, *Strategy Statement*, Stationery Office, Dublin.

Nolan, B. and T. Callan, 1992, "Cross-national poverty comparisons using relative poverty lines", in T. M. Smeeding, editor, *International Comparisons of Economic Inequality*, Research on Economic Inequality, 3, pp.277-309, JAI Press, Greenwich.

Nolan, B. and T. Callan, 1994, editors, *Poverty and Policy in Ireland*, Gill and Macmillan, Dublin.

Nolan, B. and B. Farrell, 1990, *Child Poverty in Ireland*, Combat Poverty Agency, Dublin.

Nolan, B. and C. T. Whelan, 1996, *Resources, Deprivation, and Poverty*, Clarendon Press, Oxford.

Nordisk Ministerråd, 1996, *Den nordiska fatigdoens utveckling och struktur*, TemaNord, Copenhagen.

Ó Cinnéide, S., 1972, "The extent of poverty in Ireland", *Social Studies*, 1, pp.381-400.

Ó Cinnéide, S., 1980, "Poverty and inequality in Ireland" in V. George, and R. Lawson, editors, *Poverty and Inequality in Common Market Countries*, Routledge and Kegan Paul, London.

Parker, H., 1989, *Instead of the Dole*, Routledge, London.

Peterson, P. E. and M. C. Rom, 1990, *Welfare Magnets*, Brookings Institution, Washington DC.

Sinn, H.-W., 1990, "Tax harmonisation or tax competition in Europe?", *European Economic Review*, 34, pp.489-504.

Summary of Submissions on the National Anti-Poverty Strategy, 1995, Department of An Taoiseach, Dublin.

Synthèses, 1995, *Revenus et Patrimoine des Ménages*, INSEE, Paris.

Townsend, P., 1979, *Poverty in the United Kingdom*, Allen Lane, Harmondsworth.

Vos, K. de and A. Zaidi, 1995, "Trend analysis of poverty in the European Community", Erasmus University, Rotterdam and Economics Institute, Tilburg.

Good News from Ireland:
A Geographical Perspective

Paul R. Krugman
Massachusetts Institute of Technology

E64   F43
O52

1   Introduction

Although there is no hard statistical evidence to confirm their suspicion, many people I know privately believe that favourable treatment by the business press is a sign of imminent disaster, that one should always sell the stock of any company whose CEO graces the cover of *Fortune* or *Business Week*. By this criterion, Ireland should be very worried: in the last few months the country has been the subject of almost adulatory stories in many publications, with *The Economist* actually declaring it "Europe's tiger economy". Yet the achievements are indeed remarkable. In modern Europe, a growth rate of 3 percent for a single year is cause for celebration; for the past decade Ireland has consistently managed to grow at an annual rate of 5 percent. The country's unemployment rate is still in double digits, but it has steadily fallen while that of continental Europe has steadily risen.

What went right for Ireland? This essay does not even pretend to offer a full answer to that question. What it does, instead, is to offer a few notes on the role of Ireland in the European economy; on the ways in which the character of world trade and economic geography have changed, ways that may have worked to Ireland's advantage; and on possible other reasons for Ireland's success.

2   What Kind of Economy is Ireland?

Any attempt to make sense of Ireland's success must begin with an effort to decide what is important. What things should we look at? Should we look at macroeconomic indicators like budget and trade balances, inflation and unit labour costs? Or should we look at things like the business climate, the success of Ireland in attracting multinational corporations, and so on?

Let me offer a suggestion: that there are two quite different ways of looking at an economy's performance, which will depend on how you view it. If you view it as a *national* economy, something like the economy of the United States, you will focus on one set of criteria; if you view it as a *regional* economy, something like, say, metropolitan Boston, you will want to focus on some quite different criteria.

2.1 *Nations Versus Regions*

Suppose that you want to forecast the growth of the US economy, and of living standards within that economy, over the next 15 years. You can make a pretty good prediction about the size of the labour force: leaving immigration on one side, all of those who will be working are already on site. If past US experience is any guide, actual employment will probably track the growth in that labour force pretty well. Your major uncertainty will be about the growth in productivity; that growth in productivity will determine almost everything else about the economy.

What about other things, like success in developing new export markets, breaking into new technologies, attracting foreign investment, and so on? The short answer is that while such things matter, from the point of view of the US economy they don't matter very much - or if they do matter they do so only insofar as they affect productivity growth.

Suppose, for example, that the United States does a very good job of breaking into emerging markets, boosting its exports. This will not have much if any effect on total employment, which is limited essentially by concerns about inflation rather than lack of demand. Higher exports will lead to a stronger dollar, which will mean cheaper imports; but because imports are only around 13 percent of GDP, this will add only a small amount to purchasing power. To a very good approximation, productivity is the only thing that matters. And it doesn't really matter where productivity gains are made: productivity gains in industries that compete on world markets are no more valuable than those in, say, the retail sector.

Now change focus, and ask about the prospects for growth in a particular region of the United States, such as metropolitan Boston. We may immediately say that the future growth of Boston is much more uncertain than that of the United States as a whole, because the labour force is no longer a given: workers may flood in, as they are doing at the moment, or leave, as they did in the depressed late 1980s. Productivity growth is important, but needs to be treated with some care: because Boston is a high-tech centre, it normally has higher productivity growth than other cities, but passes the benefits of that growth on to other cities in the form of lower prices.

What, then, do economists trying to forecast growth in Boston (or any other metropolitan area) look at? The usual answer is that they look at the prospects for the region's 'export base', the industries that sell to customers outside the region itself. In the case of Boston these industries include computers and software, biotechnology, higher education, and sophisticated medical care. Collectively the 'export' industries of metropolitan Boston probably employ no more than one-quarter of the labour force; but the rest of the local economy in effect exists to serve that export base. Indeed, projections of regional growth are commonly made using a "base-multiplier" model in which non-base jobs are taken as derived from the base via a more or less Keynesian multiplier process.

Why does regional economics look so different from national economics? There are two main reasons. First, the economy of a region is typically far more open to and dependent on external trade than that of a nation. We do not have statistics on the trade of Boston with the rest of the world, but a good guess is that its exports, like that of a city-state such as Singapore or Hong Kong, are considerably greater than its gross product (alias the value added on site). Even more important, factors of production - especially labour - move much more freely into and out of a regional economy than they do in most national economies. Thus if Boston is successful in capturing a pre-eminent position in, say, biotechnology, this will draw in skilled workers in that industry, and indirectly draw in workers to provide services to those biotech workers (and to each other - hence the multiplier effect).

It seems, then, that when trying to forecast or for that matter explain economic performance we use very different criteria for national economies and for the regions that comprise those national economies. At the national level it is all macroeconomics - and mainly productivity. At the regional level we tend to ask questions about industry structure and competitive position.

But what should one do when trying to make sense of the economic performance of a country like Ireland? Ireland is a sovereign state, but its population is only about two-thirds that of metropolitan Boston (at least using the extensive definition of the region). Exports are now about 80 percent of GDP, some 7 times the ratio for the United States. Should we, then, think of Ireland as a region rather than a nation?

2.2 Ireland as a European Region

In terms of size and, by and large, in terms of its dependence on trade, Ireland's economy really does look more like that of a region than that of a large country. However, the really crucial difference between regions and nations is labour mobility. The growth of the Boston economy is mainly a function of its export base, because that export base will determine the size of its labour force. The growth of the US economy is almost entirely a function of its productivity, because the size of the labour force may be taken almost as a given.

By this criterion even many quite small countries do *not* look like regional economies. The Netherlands may have only half the population of California, but California can shed excess workers through emigration, or cure a labour shortage through immigration, in a way that the Netherlands cannot. Employment in the Netherlands is therefore a macroeconomic issue, governed mainly by the same rules that apply to much larger countries.

Ireland, however, may be thought of as occupying a sort of halfway position. For one thing, the long tradition of emigration - coupled with the fact that the country shares a language both with its closest neighbour and with the United States - means that the size of Ireland's labour force is more responsive to economic conditions than that of most other countries. There is also a more subtle point: the nature of Ireland's still-high unemployment. At one time Ireland, like most of

41

Europe, was doubtless suffering from a severe case of Eurosclerosis: high unemployment was made inevitable by bad incentives in the labour market. At this point, however, the structural situation has improved (more on that below), so that at least some of the unemployment that remains is probably simply a matter of inadequate demand. But this means that successful export sectors can draw workers out of that pool of surplus labour, with much the same effect as if the economy were able to draw workers in from other regions.

It would be going too far to think of Ireland as if it were purely a regional economy, its growth driven by its export base. The kinds of macroeconomic issues that matter for bigger national economies also matter for Ireland, and must be discussed. But by moving back and forth between thinking of Ireland as a productivity-driven national economy and as an export-driven regional economy we may be able to get a fuller picture.

3   The Macroeconomic Picture

Even a quick look at the macroeconomic statistics makes one of the roots of Irish success fairly obvious: Ireland has achieved relatively fast productivity growth, without a comparable increase in wages.

Between 1979 and 1995 labour productivity in Ireland's business sector rose 3.3 percent per year - more than twice as fast as the G7 average. Meanwhile, real wages, although rising, lagged: the share of capital in business income rose sharply, from an average of 22 percent in the 1970s to 33 percent in 1995. And although Irish productivity was steadily gaining on that of richer European nations, its relative wages were not (at least partly as the result of a successful incomes policy): compensation per hour in French and German manufacturing were 50 and 100 percent higher, respectively, in the mid 1990s - about the same ratios as in the mid 1970s.

Given the combination of good productivity growth and wage restraint, the success of the economy is in a macro sense not hard to explain. With labour relatively inexpensive, the incentives were in place both for high rates of investment and for those investors to choose employment-creating rather than labour-saving techniques of production - a sharp contrast to what was happening in continental Europe. Also, given the depressed state of the European economy (especially since 1991), Ireland's steady decline in relative unit labour costs has amounted to a de facto devaluation, making its exports increasingly competitive and therefore stimulating demand for Irish products at a time when demand elsewhere in Europe was stagnant.

The big question, of course, is why productivity has grown so rapidly. The honest truth is that despite decades of work, economists still are not too good at explaining differences in national productivity performance; MIT's Robert Solow famously remarked, in the context of a discussion of Great Britain's relative decline during the 20th century, that such explanations usually end in "a blaze of amateur sociology". Ireland certainly has had substantial growth in inputs. The capital stock grew roughly in line with GDP; even more important, past investments in education have led to a rapid improvement in human capital, and dramatic improvements in infrastructure have probably played an important role.

To some extent, however, Ireland's favourable productivity performance is surely a result of its success in becoming the premier European host to inward foreign direct investment. (US foreign direct investment in Ireland is 50 percent higher per capita than in the UK, 6 times as high as in France or Germany). This is true in particular because the economy still appears to be somewhat "dualistic": it combines a fairly low-productivity, traditional sector with an advanced modern sector that is primarily foreign-owned. Thus the growth of that foreign-owned sector contributes in a direct way to productivity growth. So a crucial question becomes why Ireland has been so successful in attracting that foreign investment. What is it about Ireland that has made it so desirable a place for foreign firms to locate? In particular, what changes in the world economy have favoured that development?

4 The Changing Geography of the World Economy

The European Commission's 1990 report *One Market, One Money* classifies Ireland as a "peripheral" economy: because of its distance from and lack of direct road links to the continental markets that make up most of Europe's purchasing power, it has a relatively low "market potential" by conventional indices.

Historically, such peripheral regions have had a difficult time industrialising. Other things being the same, producers want good access both to markets and to supplies of intermediate goods; this sort of access is normally best for plants located centrally. Indeed, it has often been argued that modern economies tend to spontaneously develop a core-periphery pattern of development through a kind of circular logic: firms want to locate close to large markets, but markets tend to be large precisely where many firms choose to locate. This kind of circular logic is undoubtedly a major explanation of the historical concentration of US manufacturing in the 'manufacturing belt' of the Northeast and inner Midwest; it is probably at least a partial explanation of the concentration of European manufacturing in the 'hot banana' that stretches from Liverpool to Prague.

Ireland's recent experience, however, seems to defy this logic. In a number of industries, producers have decided to establish a single plant or facility serving the European market - but have then chosen to locate that facility in Ireland. Why don't the apparent geographical disadvantages of Ireland count more heavily in this decision - and what are the offsetting advantages?

A partial answer may be that changes in both the nature of what nations trade and in how they carry out that trade has shifted the balance of geographical advantage in a way that is favourable to Ireland. Let us therefore look briefly at the changing character of international trade.

4.1 *The Bearable Lightness of Being*

Federal Reserve Chairman, Alan Greenspan, has a stock speech that he gives when he is required to be interesting without creating panic in the financial markets; in that speech, he points out that the gross domestic product is getting *lighter*. What he means is that while the output of advanced economies is clearly rising, the sheer amount of physical stuff they produce - the tonnage of steel, coal, lumber, and so on - is not rising at nearly the same rate. We are in some sense becoming less of a material economy.

Greenspan's observation can be confirmed quite easily with regard to the international trade of the United States (and presumably of other countries). Between 1980 and 1994 US real exports as measured by the national income accounts more than doubled; but the tonnage of goods shipped out of the country actually declined slightly.

How was this possible? Part of the answer was growing exports of services; previously virtually nontradable, services such as insurance, consulting, telecommunications and so on have become major components of world trade. Meanwhile, within the goods sector there has been a shift toward trade in goods with higher value-to-weight ratios: computers rather than coal.

The net effect is to make conventional transportation costs a steadily less important factor in limiting shipments of goods. This does not mean that distance to the market has ceased to be an important issue. However, the sheer cost of shipment has become less important compared with less tangible factors such as delivery time, communication, and personal contact.

One indicator of the growing importance of time, in particular, is the rapid growth in the use of air transportation. In 1994, a remarkable 30 percent of US exports went by air (a figure that is a bit less impressive, however, if we recall that aircraft are a major US export); less than 20 percent of imports came by air, but this represented a tripling since 1980.

This growing weightlessness of international trade, again, does not mean that market access is unimportant; it does mean that the definition of that access has changed.

4.2 *Redefining Proximity*

Distance still matters. Even in manufacturing sectors where transportation costs are negligible compared with the value of the product, firms often find that trying to serve markets from long distance poses problems. For example, a number of companies have found that their customers demand rapid delivery of highly customised products. If they try to serve a market from an overseas plant, they can only meet this demand by maintaining very large inventories; while if they have a plant closer to the market they can engage in just-in-time production instead. Thus many companies have found it cost-effective to have a plant in each major continental market - e.g. one in Europe, one in North America, and one in Asia - even though on a pure production cost basis it might have seemed optimal to put all production in Southeast Asia or Latin America.

It is also true, both for manufacturers and service providers, that really long-range communication is still not as good as closer contact. Seemingly trivial things like differences in time zones, and the inability of managers to make a quick trip to discuss things in person, can add up to a serious impediment to doing business at long range.

Distance still does matter, then, but increasingly it does so because of the impediments it places on speed and ease of communication and shipment, rather than because of its impact on crude transportation cost. And this means that the 'geometry' of the world economy becomes more or less non-Euclidean. It is quite literally true that for businesses which depend on personal contact and/or rapid shipment of goods, two locations 500 miles apart but close to major airports with frequent direct flights are effectively closer to each other than two locations on opposite sides of the same large metropolitan area.

The American journalist Joel Garreau, author of *Edge City: Life on the New Frontier*, has distilled the results of interviews with businessmen into a set of tongue-in-cheek 'laws' of location. One of his laws concerns 'backshop' locations - that is, locations that perform office work that does not require continuous face-to-face contact with top management: "the maximum desirable distance a backshop location can be from a corporate headquarters: One and a half hours by car, or three hours, non-stop, by plane". The reason for these limitations is, of course, that while it does not require constant face-to-face contact, the backshop must be available for personal contact on fairly short notice - in effect, must be reachable by a long day trip or quick overnighter.

The point is that many producers of traded goods and services are starting to resemble backshops: they either do not produce a physical product at all, or produce a good with such a high value-to-weight ratio that transportation costs are not important; but because of the sophistication of the product and the need for close interaction with customers, they must be produced in locations easily accessible when necessary.

4.3 *Ireland as an Export Platform*

We can now return to the situation of Ireland. It seems apparent that the changed rules of market access have, it turns out, worked very much in Ireland's favour. On one side, for many industries really long-range, intercontinental trade is still not an option: they still have strong incentives to serve European markets from a European location. So Ireland is not in competition with Asia or Mexico for these industries. On the other side, since crude transport cost considerations have been replaced with more subtle issues of communication and personal contact, Ireland's insular location and distance from continental markets matter much less than they used to. In particular, Ireland easily meets Garreau's criteria for a 'backshop' with regard to virtually all of the European Union.

In the United States many companies have chosen to locate backshops a thousand or more miles from headquarters, in pursuit of lower office and wage costs; Ireland is closer to major European markets than that, and the wage differential vis-a-vis advanced continental countries is vastly larger than any differentials in North America. When one adds the highly favourable tax treatment of profits in manufacturing and tradable services, it should not be surprising that Ireland is attractive as an export platform.

What remains surprising is that it has done so much better than other 'peripheral' economies. Labour costs in Spain are similar to those in Ireland; those in Portugal and Greece are far lower. Yet foreign investment into those economies has been substantially lower. True, in the case of the really low-wage countries lack of infrastructure and poor access to the markets limit their usefulness as export platforms. And there is, of course, the huge advantage that comes from the availability of a work force that is not only well-educated but English-speaking. Nonetheless, it is worth discussing at least briefly some reasons why Ireland has been uniquely successful in taking advantage of the changing shape of economic geography.

5 Self-Reinforcing Success?

Episodes of rapid regional growth are fairly common within national economies. Typically they occur when a region succeeds, through some combination of policy and sheer luck, in developing a self-reinforcing industrial cluster. While such self-reinforcing growth often occurs in high-technology manufacturing industries like semiconductors or biotechnology, it can also occur in production of low-tech goods like toys (currently surging in Los Angeles), non-material goods like software, and services like insurance.

Ireland's boom has many of the elements of a typical regional economic takeoff, together with some interesting dynamics related to the uncertainties of foreign investment.

5.1 *External Economies*

The classic 'external economy' explanation of industrial clusters, advanced by Alfred Marshall more than a century ago, identified three basic reasons why a local concentration of an industry is often self-reinforcing. First, a cluster of related producers may support local suppliers of specialised inputs subject to economies of scale. Second, such a cluster provides a thick labour market for people with specialised skills, offering workers a better chance of finding new jobs if their employer does badly and simultaneously offering firms a better chance of expanding rapidly if they discover unexpected opportunities. Finally, a local industrial clustering encourages spillovers of information.

These advantages are often hard to pin down. Nonetheless, it seems clear that Ireland has developed some more or less classic Marshallian clusters, especially in the electronics and pharmaceutical industries. Promotional literature from the Industrial Development Authority stresses the availability of high-quality specialist services (e.g. clean room and sterilisation), and of a pool of workers with the requisite skills. Technological spillovers are harder to demonstrate, but given the clustering in high technology industries seem likely.

A first-pass view of the Irish foreign direct investment boom, then, might see it as more or less comparable to the growth of Silicon Valley: due to some combination of good policy and sheer luck, Ireland beat out other possible sites in developing a critical mass of firms in sectors subject to external economies; from then on new entrants chose Ireland as a site because of the advantages conveyed by its existing concentration, and in so doing reinforced those advantages. Again, it is worth bearing in mind that Ireland, if it were a metropolitan area, would rank only 12th in the United States; there is no reason why an 'Irish miracle' could not result from the same sort of forces that produced the 'Massachusetts miracle' of the 1980s, a classic example of a boom (unfortunately, a short-lived one) based on external economies that gave a regional economy an advantage in a rapidly growing industrial cluster.

However, one might guess that there is a bit more to it than that - that there are some dynamic aspects which are special to a country as opposed to a regional economy within the United States, and which help explain why Ireland has done well in at least four seemingly unrelated industrial sectors.

5.2 *Demonstration Effects and Cascades*

Firms considering opening production facilities in other countries, to a considerably greater extent than those remaining at home, face uncertainties about how well the operations will actually run. Sometimes they are agreeably surprised: a factory in a low-wage country may turn out to be very nearly as efficient as a comparable factory at home. Other times the surprise is unpleasant: even what seem like cut-and-dried operations can sometimes turn out to be far less efficient in a country with unreliable workers, infrastructure, and so on.

In these circumstances firms have a strong incentive to observe each others' decisions, and where possible experience, even if there is no direct linkage between those decisions. And this mutual observation can cause a tendency for investment to concentrate in a few destinations, over and above the usual external economy arguments.

Suppose, to make things a bit more concrete, that there are a number of US-based firms considering opening European operations. They are reasonably sure that they should choose a country that trades off a less-central location for somewhat lower wages - so they are deciding between Ireland and Spain. What they do not know is how well things will actually work out in each country.

Now suppose that for whatever reason several firms choose to locate in Ireland - and their experience is favourable. Then other firms will have a strong incentive to follow their lead. It is not that they *know* that Ireland is a better site than Spain. But they know that Ireland is better than expected, and they do not have that information about Spain. And it is not in the interest of any individual firm to get that information! In other words, investors may, entirely rationally, end up 'following the herd' based on the demonstration effect of a few successful leaders.

In fact, such herding can develop even before the results of the first wave of investment are in. Imagine two firms A and B, each with independent information about the relative merits of Ireland and Spain, but each also knowing that the other may know things it does not. Suppose that firm A chooses Ireland. This demonstrates that its information suggests that Ireland is a better location. If firm B's own information offers no clear advantage to Spain, it will be wise to emulate A, figuring that it knew something. In fact, even if B's information seems more favourable to Spain, it will still rationally choose Ireland unless that information is sufficiently strong to overrule the evidence that someone else arrived at a different conclusion. If there is a firm C, it will look at the decisions of both A and B to choose Ireland and be very reluctant to trust its own judgement even if its own analysis favours Spain; and so on. In other words, even aside from the demonstration effects of early success, early decisions about the location of investment can produce a cascade of followers.

All this can be put in common-sense terms. Consider an American company that has decided to establish a European facility. It knows that other American companies have done well in Ireland, while other possible locations do not have a track record; unless there is clear evidence that another site would in fact be even better, the company will simply take advantage of that information. Moreover, the fact that other companies have chosen Ireland suggests that their research pointed to the superiority of an Irish site; the company is likely to question the results of its own research if it comes to a different conclusion.

In short, quite aside from external economies, success can breed success. This is not entirely a matter of chance: if Ireland did not appear to be an attractive production site it would not have attracted the first wave of investors, and if it had not delivered on that promise it would not have been able to maintain its advantage. But one could imagine an alternative history in which early choices happened to go to other countries (e.g. to Portugal with its very low wages, or for that matter to the United Kingdom), and in which the cascade in Ireland never got started. Fortunately, Ireland got off on the right foot.

6   Some Risks

The Irish success story may be briefly summarised as follows: a decade ago Ireland, despite its debt and unemployment problems, had some strong points: a well-educated population, enough social cohesion to introduce an effective incomes policy that kept wages low compared with continental Europe, and the fact that its work force speaks English. An opportunity was then presented as a result of changes in the underlying geography of the world economy: as trade became less influenced by transportation costs but more critically dependent on communication, a location within Europe became necessary but one in the centre of Europe less important. Thanks in part to luck, in part to policies (including investments in telecommunications), Ireland got a head start over other European locations in attracting what became a surge of inward foreign direct investment; the early investments both generated a cascade through informational effects and, eventually, created external economies that further reinforced Ireland's advantages.

So far this process seems if anything to be accelerating. At some point, of course, Ireland will begin to run up against the constraint of limited labour supply. But beyond that, are there important risks to the continuation of the Irish miracle? Let us consider three.

First, to the extent that Ireland's success resembles regional booms like the Massachusetts miracle of the 1980s, it is vulnerable to shifts in technology. Right now, Ireland is prospering from a phase of globalisation that turns out to be 'just right' for its geographical situation: distance matters much less than it used to, but by and large firms still want to serve the European market from a European location. At the moment this situation seems likely to persist for some time: time zones are not about to go away, and while air travel may get cheaper it appears unlikely to get significantly faster for the foreseeable future. Basically, an overnight trip from Dublin to Frankfurt is easy, while one from Kuala Lumpur to Frankfurt will be impossible for a long time to come. However, it is possible to imagine changes in the world - for example, improvements in the technology and social acceptability of video-conferencing - that might vitiate the advantages of a European location.

A second, perhaps less speculative, threat lies in the possibility that other European locations may begin to compete more effectively for the role of export platform. One might note in particular that some of the Eastern European countries have large numbers of highly technically trained people, available at very low wage rates. At the moment lack of infrastructure and political uncertainty hold back exploitation of that resource; but this could change, and could pose a threat to Ireland's special advantages.

Finally, there is the question of Ireland's role within a Europe that seems increasingly uncertain of its direction. Ireland has built its economic success on being a gateway to Europe, and until recently was also a major recipient of aid; politically, Ireland has at least seemed to stand with the 'federalisers' who want a more powerful Brussels, and against the Euroskeptic tendencies of the United Kingdom. However, with growing economic tension within Europe, Ireland is actually in a somewhat vulnerable position. There is a growing contrast between the high-wage, high-unemployment countries of the continent and the lower-wage, lower-unemployment UK economy. One response of at least some on the continent is to make charges of 'social dumping', in effect blaming part of their unemployment on the more liberal labour market policies of their neighbours.

To date Ireland has largely managed to stand on the sidelines of this fig
because it is so small, partly because it does not have an aggressive free-ı
ideology. Nonetheless, at some point one can all too easily imagine Freı
politicians noticing that Ireland pays wages well below the EU average, taxes
capital far less than other European states, and that partly because of those low
wages and taxes it has become a favourite export platform for non-European
firms serving the European market. If Brussels ever does start to impose rules
aimed at preventing social dumping, they would probably bite even more
severely on Ireland than on the UK.

Even taking into account these risks, however, Ireland appears to be in an
enviable position. Through a combination of good luck, good timing, and good
policies, it has caught the crest of a geographical and technological wave, and it
has ridden it to a prosperity nobody expected.

Ireland's Growth Strategy :
...ons for Economic Development

Jeffrey D. Sachs
Harvard Institute for International Development

052
047 F43

1 Ireland's Rapid Growth

During the 1990s, Ireland has been the most successful economy of the European Union, and indeed the fastest growing country among the members of the Organisation for Economic Cooperation and Development (OECD), the association of advanced economies. During 1991-96, Ireland achieved average annual growth in per capita GDP (adjusted for purchasing power parity) of 5.5%, well above the average per capita growth of the other 14 countries of the European Union, 1.7% per year. In 1996, Ireland was one of the fastest growing economies in the world, with a per capita growth rate of 6.6%. The ratio of employment to the total labour force (sometimes termed the employment rate) also rose, signifying the strong increase in job growth during the same years. The employment rate rose by 2.2 percentage points between 1991 and 1996, compared with an average *fall* in the employment rate of 0.7 percentage points in the other 14 European Union economies.

To some extent, Ireland's rapid growth is an example of convergence, the empirical regularity in which relatively lower income economies grow more rapidly than the relatively richer economies. The lagging economies have opportunities for 'catching up' through the importation of technology and capital, and through high returns on domestic investments. Among the OECD economies in the post-war period, the tendency towards convergence has been strong. But something else is surely taking place, since Ireland has strongly out paced the even poorer countries of Southern Europe, such as Greece, Portugal and Spain. Also, the tendency towards convergence is far from automatic. Rapid growth in lagging countries depends on a set of economic, political, and social institutions which support the catching-up process.

A useful reference point for understanding Ireland's performance is that of the East Asian tigers, especially the smaller countries such as Hong Kong and Singapore, and the interesting case of Malaysia. Ireland in recent years has followed a kind of East Asian growth strategy, basing rapid growth on manufacturing exports made possible through large inflows of foreign direct investment (FDI). Even Ireland's main locus of manufacturing export growth, electronics, is common to the East Asian tigers. There are a shared set of policies and institutions - especially in taxation, trade, international finance, labour markets - that have enabled small economies such as Ireland and the East Asian tigers to attract large-scale FDI for the purpose of export promotion. As East Asia and Ireland have shown, such a strategy can provide a basic policy framework for small economies to promote rapid catching-up growth.

Ireland, however, still faces important economic risks in the future. While Ireland shares many of the fast-growth elements of the East Asian tigers, it also continues to share many of the slow-growth elements of the European Union. Standing astride two economic models - Asian-style export-led growth and EU-style social welfarism - Ireland could still get stuck in the slow-growth, high-unemployment trap of most of its fellow EU nations. Ireland will require a clear understanding of the sources of its recent successes if it is to steer clear of the risks ahead.

2   Small Economies and Export-Led Growth

For a country on the scale of Ireland, with some 3.6 million people, the only path to prosperity is a deep integration with larger markets. First, Ireland's domestic economy is too small to support a highly differentiated industrial base, especially in sectors with significant economies of scale such as steel or automobiles. To achieve economic efficiency, Ireland has to specialise in particular niches of tradable industries, relying on imports to supply a wide range of industrial needs, both for final goods as well as for machinery and intermediate inputs. Second, traditional infant-industry arguments in favour of *temporary* import protection as a source of long-term export promotion, dubious as these arguments usually are even for the largest economies, are completely inappropriate for smaller economies such as Ireland. The domestic market is simply too small to support a competitive and efficient market environment for most industrial products, or to provide much benefit for domestic firms that will have to rely mainly on international markets. Third, small economies can develop domestically only a very small fraction of the modern technologies needed to support an advanced economy. Thus, Ireland and indeed almost all other countries in the world need to rely heavily on the importation of world-class technologies to achieve world-class living standards. These technologies are often embedded in capital goods that are imported for the sake of domestic production.

Given the structural constraints facing a small economy such as Ireland, high income levels depend on successful export-led growth. Moreover, even within its specialised export sectors, Ireland will have to rely heavily on inflows of foreign technology. The smaller East Asian tigers, such as Singapore, Hong Kong, and the special trading zones of Malaysia (e.g. Penang Island), have demonstrated a successful model of export-led growth based on large-scale foreign direct investment (FDI) flows into niche export sectors. The FDI serves three main purposes: it links domestic production with world-class technological leaders, who provide technologies and detailed specifications for global production; it provides foreign saving to augment domestic saving; and it offers marketing outlets for the domestic production through the marketing channels of the multinational firms. Interestingly and notably, the Asian tiger niche export markets were heavily concentrated in electronics production. This is the same sector that has dominated export-led growth in Ireland.

The creation of FDI-based export-led growth requires that domestic policy create an investor friendly environment for export-driven FDI. Conditions for high profitability of FDI include:

• low rates of corporate taxation, or special tax incentives for foreign investment in targeted sectors;

• liberal policies on foreign direct investment inflows, including 100% ownership of domestic operations by foreign owners;

- low or zero tariff duties on the importation of capital goods and intermediate products used in the production of the export sector;

- a competitive exchange rate to maintain internationally competitive wage levels (adjusting wages for labour productivity);

- adequate provision of infrastructure (power, ports, warehousing) and efficient administrative services (customs, taxation) to insure an efficient interface between domestic production and world markets;

- a stable political environment, free of concerns over expropriation or unstable government regulation;

- low rates of government expenditure as a share of GDP, making possible low rates of taxation;

- a competitive labour market, with low rates of distortionary labour taxation (e.g. payroll taxes), low or no minimum wages, and flexibility in the recruitment and dismissal of workers;

- favourable geography, supporting low transport costs for shipments from suppliers and delivery to main export markets.

Almost by definition, countries competing for export-oriented FDI are in a tough market in which footloose industries searching for cost advantages can choose among many alternative locations. Moreover, in a sector such as electronics, domestic production might cover only a small part of the overall value of final output. For example, a country such as Malaysia has specialised in the assembly and testing of semiconductor components, and the assembly of circuit boards using imported components. The import content of final exports can easily be more than half, and even up to 90% of the final export value. In this case, even small duties on imports, or modest excessive charges in transport costs of intermediate inputs can render a country internationally uncompetitive. FDI will simply shift to another location. Thus, FDI-led export growth requires a taut discipline in domestic economic policy in order to keep the country attractive as an investment site.

3   Ireland's Success in FDI-Based Export Promotion

Ireland's strategy for successful export-led growth has taken time to bring to fruition. Despite some obvious 'structural' constraints on a small economy such as Ireland, the country has been subject to long periods in which policy makers erroneously looked to the stimulus of the internal market as the engine of growth. The most famous phase in modern history was 1932-57, when Ireland launched a policy of import-substituting industrialisation in the depths of the Depression. The notoriety of Ireland's policy was magnified by John Maynard Keynes' endorsement of the inward-looking strategy in his famous Finlay Lecture on "Economic Self-Sufficiency" delivered at University College, Dublin in April 1933[1]. The policy, in retrospect was a debacle. For example, during 1949-56, in the years just before the abandonment of the policy, "Irish national income grew just 8% compared to 21% in Britain and 40% in continental Europe".[2]

After 1958, Ireland turned towards export promotion, based heavily on the attraction of foreign direct investment. Gradually, Ireland began to put in place important cuts in corporate tax rates and other inducements to capital inflows. But even with the new strategy in mind, Irish policy makers and politicians remained of two minds: on the one hand attempting to create a highly competitive environment for export-oriented FDI aimed at the European market, and on the other the creation of a European-style social welfare state built upon generous government benefits and high levels of government expenditure. The policy regime oscillated between these two often inconsistent goals. Export competitiveness required a lean state and low levels of taxation; the social welfare ambitions constantly put pressure on the fisc and drove up tax rates other than on corporate capital.

---

[1] Sixty-one years later, I had the honour to deliver the re-named Finlay O'Brien Lectures in the very same lecture hall at University College. Upon re-reading Keynes' lecture on this occasion, I found Keynes' temporary abandonment of his lifelong commitment to open trade to be muddled and unconvincing as economics, but powerful as a measure of Keynes' despair in the depths of the Great Depression.

[2] Jacobsen, John Kurt, 1994, *Chasing Progress in the Irish Republic: Ideology, Democracy, and Dependent Development*, Cambridge University Press, Cambridge, p.54.

The 1980s witnessed a severe fiscal crisis following a period during which the Irish Government had wrongheadedly gone for growth on the basis of increased fiscal expenditure. Government spending reached more than 50% of GDP in the early 1980s, while the budget deficit soared to 13% of GDP in 1982. Public debt sky-rocketed, with gross financial liabilities of the general government jumping from 70% of GDP in 1979 to an astounding 116% of GDP in 1987. A 1986 report of the National Economic and Social Council described the situation as "almost unremittingly grim", requiring "a radical change of policy".[3]

Ireland's rapid growth was put on course through dramatic cutbacks in government expenditure as a percent of GDP beginning in the late 1980s. Total government outlays fell sharply from 51% of GDP in 1987 to 43% of GDP in 1993. This brought down the financial imbalance of the general government from a deficit of 8.5% of GDP in 1987 to a deficit of just 2.4% of GDP in 1993. Government financial liabilities as a share of GDP also fell accordingly, from 116% in 1987 to a still high 97% in 1993. The great lesson from this fiscal retrenchment, however, was that lower levels of government expenditure as a percent of GDP supported a surge in export-led growth. While the GDP increased at an annual rate of 2.3% between 1982 and 1987, growth increased to 4.5% between 1987 and 1993. It has, of course, been even faster since 1993, averaging around 7.0% per year between 1993 and 1996.

The successful fiscal turnaround and acceleration of GDP after 1987 exemplify the patterns of FDI-based export-led growth. Ireland, together with Scotland, became the locations of choice within the European Community for inward-looking direct investments in high-technology electronics firms. Ireland's Silicon Bog, as it came to be known, has attracted the leading names in global electronics - Ericsson, Hewlett-Packard, Motorola, Siemens, Sun Microsystems, Westinghouse, to name a few. The share of exports in GDP rose from around 65% in 1984 to 77% in 1993, reflecting compound growth of exports (at constant prices) of around 9% per annum.

---

[3] Cited in Jacobsen, 1994, p.170.

Recent studies of the Harvard Institute for International Development, in conjunction with the 1997 Global Competitiveness Report (GCR) of the World Economic Forum, underscore the specific institutional and structural factors which have favoured the rapid growth of Ireland's exports and GDP. Relative to most EU countries, Ireland stands out in four crucial dimensions: labour markets; corporate taxation; exchange rate policy; and technology transfer via foreign direct investment. Favourable policies in these areas, together with strong performance on other aspects of economic management (e.g. macroeconomic stability, rule of law, openness of trade), contributed to Ireland's high ranking in overall competitiveness compared with most other European Union countries. In 1997, Ireland ranked 16th out of 53 countries surveyed by the World Economic Forum, coming in fourth place among the European Union economies, behind the UK (7th), Luxembourg (11th), and Netherlands (12th), but way ahead of the rest of the EU, including France (23rd), Germany (25th), Italy (39th), Portugal (30th) and Spain (26th).

Table 1 shows a more detailed breakdown of Ireland's sources of competitive strengths and weaknesses in comparison with the continental European Union countries (note that all rankings are out of a complete tally of 53 countries in the GCR). Ireland is judged to be more competitive than continental Europe (in the precise sense of having institutions more conducive to long-term growth) in six sub-categories, openness, government, technology, management, labour, and institutions, and about the same rank in two, finances and infrastructure. In essence, Ireland is seen to be more efficient in labour market institutions, more open (and with a more realistic exchange rate policy in recent years), and less burdened by very high levels of government expenditure, than the social welfare states in continental Europe. Also, the business executives confirm the extent of technology transfer and management quality that has accompanied the inflow of high-tech foreign investment into Ireland. Of course, these results are not grounds for complacency. After all, Ireland still ranks fairly far from the top of the list, with particular gaps seen in financial markets and in the quality of infrastructure. And while Ireland's fiscal policy is more growth-oriented than the rest of the European Union, it is nonetheless less growth-promoting than in many other parts of the world, where tax rates and levels of government expenditure are a much smaller proportion of the gross domestic product.

Table 1 Competitiveness Rankings, Ireland and the European Union

	Ireland	European Union
Overall Ranking	16	27
Openness	9	20
Government	22	42
Finances	29	26
Infrastructure	23	24
Technology	6	22
Management	11	20
Labour	19	38
Institutions	11	17

Note: All rankings are on a scale of 1 (highest) to 53 (lowest). European Union refers to the average of continental EU countries except Luxembourg.
Source: *1997 Global Competitiveness Report*, World Economic Forum, and Harvard Institute for International Development.

On specific responses to the executive surveys carried out by the World Economic Forum, Ireland's minimum wage regulations are *not* deemed to be important barriers to hiring unskilled or young workers, in contrast with the situation in other EU countries. Similarly, Ireland's labour market regulations are *not* seen as seriously impeding the adjustment of labour hours to fluctuations in demand, at least in comparison with other EU countries. In short, Ireland's labour markets are seen as more responsive to market conditions than in other EU countries. The situation is obviously far from ideal, however, in view of Ireland's chronically high unemployment rates. With regard to taxation, Ireland's overall tax burden is moderate when compared with the very high tax burdens elsewhere in the European Union. With regard to exchange rate policy, Ireland's exchange rate policy is judged by the business executives to be supportive of export expansion, in contrast with other European Union countries where overly strong currencies are deemed to be inimical to export growth. Ireland's devaluation in 1993 helped to preserve overall exchange rate competitiveness within the European Exchange Rate Mechanism.

In summary, Ireland's recent experience as a fast-growing economy offers general lessons for developing countries that are aiming at 'catch up' growth. The path to fast growth through FDI-linked, high-technology exports has been demonstrated not only by Ireland, Scotland, and several high-performing economies of East Asia, but recently by a widening circle of other developing countries. In 1996, for example, Costa Rica successfully competed (reportedly against Malaysia, Ireland and Mexico) for a major new Intel semiconductor facility, which promises to nearly double Costa Rica's total exports within five years. To win the bid, Costa Rica had to demonstrate the same conditions of competitiveness that have supported Ireland's growth in recent years: openness to FDI, suitable infrastructure, favourable tax conditions and other arrangements necessary for profitability (e.g. duty-free access to imported intermediate and capital goods used in the production process).

4 Maintaining High Growth in Ireland

Ireland's status as a high-growth dynamo in Europe is built on significant foundations, but it is still far from secure in the long term. Ireland's policies, I noted at the outset, have long been of two minds: export competitiveness as one imperative, matched by attraction to large-scale social welfare spending as an alternative model. While Ireland's government spending as a per cent of GDP is moderate compared with most of the European Union, it is actually very high compared with the fast-growing countries of East Asia. The ratio of total expenditures to GDP now hovers around 45% in Ireland, compared with 15% in Hong Kong, 24% in Singapore, 35% in Malaysia, and 30% in Taiwan. As a result, the East Asian tigers have been able to maintain a range of key taxes at much lower rates than in Ireland. This is true, for example, in the important areas of personal income taxation and payroll taxation. Ireland's top marginal tax rate on personal income reaches 48%, while payroll taxes (PRSI, or pay-related social insurance contributions) range up to 18.75%. The top marginal income tax rate in Hong Kong, by contrast, is just 20%, and is 30% in Singapore. There are no payroll taxes in Hong Kong, and in Singapore, pension contributions are in the form of mandatory payments to individualised saving accounts rather than taxes for government revenue. This kind of individualised provident fund system is also in operation in Malaysia.

One of Ireland's tasks in the years ahead will be to reduce gradually the burden of government expenditure and taxation. Cutbacks in government spending will not be easy, especially since much of government spending falls on politically charged areas of social policy, such as health and retirement pensions. As mentioned above, Singapore and Malaysia have avoided large and expensive budgetary outlays through innovative state-managed systems of mandatory household saving. The Provident Funds in these countries ensure that households have retirement protection, while at the same time limiting the state's role in the *direct provision* of retirement benefits. It is likely that Ireland (and the rest of the European Union) will have to explore such mechanisms for state-regulated private financing in the future, if rapid economic growth is to be maintained while meeting the social objectives of the nation.

There is another risk to Ireland's export-led growth model. Ireland must maintain cost competitiveness, with changes in wage levels appropriately reflecting changes in productivity and world demand for Ireland's products. In the past, Ireland has used exchange rate devaluations to restore cost competitiveness at times when domestic costs got out of line. If Europe indeed moves to a single currency, and Ireland joins the system, Ireland will close the door on exchange rate flexibility as an instrument of policy. This is surely a big risk for a small country that is dependent on export-led growth, perhaps even too big a risk. In any event, if Ireland does join the single currency, it will put added urgency to enhancing Ireland's labour market flexibility as a key to maintaining cost competitiveness in international markets.

Privatisation, Regulation And Competition: Some Implications for Ireland

John S. Vickers*
All Souls College, Oxford

1 Introduction

In the eighteen years of Conservative government from 1979 to 1997, Britain conducted an instructive series of experiments in privatisation and regulatory reform. What are the main lessons of that experience for a country in Ireland's position, and for the European Union more generally?

This essay attempts to answer that question in three steps. First, it is important to set out some economic principles of privatisation, regulation and competition policy. Second, an overview is given of the British privatisation programme, and the regulatory and competitive reforms that have accompanied it, with particular attention to the telecommunications, gas and electricity industries. Third and most tentatively, some implications are drawn for Ireland as it faces the prospect of increasing EU liberalisation.

2 Economic Principles[1]

2.1 *Privatisation*

'Privatisation' is defined here as the transfer from government to private parties of the ownership of firms. This definition is not so broad as to embrace, for example, the sale of publicly owned housing and natural resources, contracting

* I am very grateful to John Fingleton, Alan W. Gray and Brendan Walsh for comments on an earlier version of this essay, but they are not implicated in any way.

[1] Parts of this section and the next draw from Vickers, 1997. I am grateful to Macmillans for permission to do this.

out the supply of publicly financed services, or the introduction of user charges for services previously provided at public expense. However, some of the economic principles for privatising firms apply more generally.

Privatisation being transfer of ownership, the first question to ask is: what is ownership? According to the incomplete contracts view of the firm (see Hart, 1995), ownership of an asset is to be identified with residual rights of control - rights to make decisions in the domain not already subject to contractual obligations. No such rights would exist in a world of complete contracts, where ownership, and hence privatisation, would therefore be irrelevant.

The ultimate owners of sizeable firms typically delegate the exercise of residual control rights to professional managers (whose identity may be unaffected by privatisation). Privatisation affects principal-agent relationships between owners and managers by changing (i) the principals and hence their objectives, (ii) the means of monitoring and giving incentives to the agents, and (iii) the scope for action by the former public principals.

As to (i), a limitation to the economic analysis of privatisation is that there is no definitive theory of the firm under public ownership. In some sense the ultimate owners are the general public, but even if their preferences could satisfactorily be aggregated into a welfare measure, it would be pious to suppose that the government ministers or officials will always necessarily exercise their authority over public firms to maximise welfare, avoiding distraction by political considerations, influence by well-organised vested interests, and so on. The usual assumption that the owners of private firms seek to maximise profit or share value seems a tolerable approximation for present purposes, except perhaps if workers or consumers have large ownership stakes.

Since private, unlike public, ownership claims are generally tradable, privatisation can alter the monitoring and incentives of managers by adding to the information base upon which incentive contracts can be written. Managers' rewards can be related to share price performance contractually or, for example, by share option schemes. Insofar as share prices reflect the value of the firm, managers can thereby be given incentives to enhance firm value. Stock market investment analysts become a new source of managerial monitoring. However, free-rider considerations imply that monitoring by private owners might be limited, especially if share ownership is diffuse.

The tradability of ownership claims also means that, unless they are given special protection, privatised firms are potentially vulnerable to takeover threats, whereas publicly-owned firms obviously are not. It is a matter for debate whether such threats from the market for corporate control are effective in disciplining managers of private firms to act in shareholder interests. Private firms also face the possibility of bankruptcy, in which case residual control rights shift to debtholders.

Privatisation changes the relationship between government and the firm. Thus public officials may lose power to intervene in the running of the firm, for example because they lose access to information about it. Insofar as they have objectives at variance with welfare, this may be directly beneficial (see Shapiro and Willig, 1990). Moreover, and perhaps most important, the credibility of government commitment not to intervene may be enhanced by privatisation so that, for example, managers face harder budget constraints and hence stronger incentives (see Schmidt, 1996).

Nevertheless, privatisation is unlikely always to make government commitment not to intervene completely credible, especially if the firm remains subject to regulation. In any event, government retains powers of taxation,[2] and ultimately there is the possibility that privatisation might be reversed, possibly on terms disadvantageous to private owners. To the extent that these factors give rise to any risk of more or less subtle expropriation by government, private investment incentives may be adversely affected.

From the considerations above it follows that the consequences of privatisation are likely to be influenced by the extent of market power enjoyed by the firm in question. For a firm that operates in competitive conditions, the shift from 'public' to profit objectives raises no concerns about the exercise of market power, and, since no special regulatory apparatus is required, opportunities for expropriation are limited. In these circumstances one may expect private ownership to be superior to public ownership in terms of economic efficiency, and indeed that is what the empirical evidence shows (see Boardman and Vining, 1989[3]).

---

[2] As illustrated by the 'windfall tax' on privatised utilities in Gordon Brown's July 1997 budget.

[3] For empirical studies of privatisation, see Galal et al, 1994, and Megginson et al, 1994.

For a firm with market power, however, it may be desirable for reasons of allocative efficiency, and inevitable for political reasons, for privatisation to be accompanied by monopoly regulation. But regulation risks blunting the very incentives - e.g. for cost reduction and efficient investment - that privatisation is usually intended to sharpen.

A complementary approach to the problem of privatised (and indeed nationalised) market power is liberalisation - i.e. the removal of legal and other barriers to competition, and accompanying measures to contain anti-competitive behaviour by the incumbent. Among other things, liberalisation may expose and undermine patterns of cross-subsidy practised under public monopoly.

Therefore, in contrast to the competitive market case, it would appear that no general claim can be made as to the economic desirability of privatising firms with market power. The accompanying regimes of regulation and competition policy are crucial determinants of the consequences of their privatisation. This conclusion is consistent with the mixed empirical evidence comparing efficiency under public and private ownership.

In addition to microeconomic efficiency, considerations of public finance have motivated privatisation policies in a number of countries, including Britain. By raising government revenue, privatisation reduces the immediate need for public sector borrowing. It may also release firms from financial constraints resulting from government macroeconomic policy commitments. Both these points require examination.

Selling public firms indeed raises government revenue, but the same is true of selling public bonds: in both cases the public sector receives a lump-sum in return for a stream of future profit or interest payments. The deeper question is how privatisation differs from government bond issue in terms of its effect on the net worth of the public sector.

If privatisation leads to economic efficiency gains - or to greater exercise of monopoly power, which is equivalent to a tax increase in public finance terms - then the firm's profits are greater with privatisation than in the public sector. If the firm is sold at a fair price, then the public sector captures the net present value of the profit gain (less the transactions costs of privatisation, which are likely to exceed those of bonds). If, however, the firm is underpriced, then any gain to the net worth of the public sector is reduced by the extent of underpricing. Competition among potential buyers and a pre-existing market for the firm's shares are factors likely to assist accurate pricing of privatisation issues.

Privatisation can also affect the net worth of the public sector, compared with selling government bonds, if risk-adjusted discount rates differ. For example, a government with poor inflationary credibility may have to cede a large interest rate premium when selling bonds. Shares in privatised firms are not so vulnerable to expropriation via inflation (neither are index-linked bonds). However, as discussed above in relation to regulatory credibility, some privatised firms, especially those with monopoly power, may face possibilities of expropriation via regulation or even renationalisation. The relative sizes of these risks of default on debt and of 'default on equity' are likely to vary by industry as well as by country. The nature of the private shareholders - e.g. their nationality or whether they are small individual investors - might also be an influence upon the probability of expropriation.

Self-imposed public finance constraints by government can provide efficiency arguments for privatisation if they prevent publicly owned firms from making desirable investments. In macroeconomic terms, it ought to matter little whether a firm is in public or private ownership when it does a given amount of borrowing, but it appears that the impact on government macroeconomic credibility can be rather different.

Privatisation, and the financial and industrial policies that accompany it, may also have large distributional consequences. First, if public firms are sold to private investors for less than their market value - for example as part of a plan to promote 'wider share ownership' - then, relative to the situation with more accurate pricing, wealth is redistributed away from the general taxpayer to the investors who succeed in getting shares. Employees and managers of privatised firms gain from such redistribution if, as has often happened in practice, they are allocated shares on favourable terms. Managers may benefit also from share option schemes and from being released from public sector pay constraints.

Second, if privatisation hardens the firm's budget constraint, then it may diminish rents enjoyed by those within the firm to the benefit of the general taxpayer. Third, widespread cross-subsidy - e.g. of small customers by large customers, and/or of suppliers of certain inputs - is a not uncommon feature of publicly owned monopoly. Privatisation entails redistribution insofar as it undoes such cross-subsidies, but, here as elsewhere, the accompanying regime of regulation and competition is likely to be at least as important. Thus liberalisation tends to be a more potent enemy of cross-subsidy than privatisation by itself, and, in the case of privatised monopoly, regulation can be a major determinant of the extent of redistribution among consumer groups as well as between consumers and shareholders.

2.2 *Regulation*

In assessing methods of monopoly regulation, it is sensible first to consider the objectives of regulation, and the fundamental reasons why their attainment is difficult. Three important economic objectives are:

- prices that reflect costs, so that users face efficient price signals and profits are neither excessive nor inadequate,
- incentives for operating cost efficiency, and
- long-term investment incentives.

However, starting from a situation with price distortions, a move towards cost-reflective pricing is unlikely to be universally popular because, in the absence of other policy measures, those who have in the past been cross-subsidised tend to lose out.

In an ideal world it might be possible simultaneously to attain the aims above, but several fundamental problems exist in practice, including:

- asymmetric information – the firm generally knows more than the government regulator about industry conditions,
- limited commitment power – the government regulator cannot credibly commit all future policies (e.g. that investors will necessarily get a decent rate of return on capital), and
- regulatory capture – the danger that vested interests (e.g. managers and employees of incumbent firms with market power) will indirectly determine regulatory policy, or at least spend considerable resources seeking to influence it.

The task of regulatory design – for private or public monopolies – is to minimise these problems so as to achieve the economic (and any other) objectives of regulation as fully as possible. The key question of monopoly price control, which is often posed as the choice between price caps and rate-of-return regulation, illustrates the issues well.

Under price cap regulation, an upper limit on the monopolist's prices (or some average of them) is fixed in advance, at least for a period of time. In consequence the firm keeps/loses all the benefit/cost of superior/inferior efficiency. This is good for incentives for operating cost efficiency, and the danger of regulatory capture seems limited because, at least on the face of it, the regulator has relatively few decisions to make. But prices and costs might come apart, with possible consequences for profit volatility. In particular, high profits might seem unfair to the public, perhaps with damaging consequences for regulatory credibility and hence investment incentives.

Rate-of-return regulation, on the other hand, keeps prices in line with costs, at least on average, and avoids excess or inadequate profit problems provided that the rate of return and capital base are properly measured (there is ample scope for dispute and influence-seeking on these issues). If rate-of-return regulation is credible, investors have few worries about receiving an adequate return. But incentives for cost minimisation are poor, since cost increases can be passed on to consumers.

In fact the differences between price cap and rate-of-return regulation are by no means as stark as this sketch may have suggested. First, price cap regulation can have explicit passthrough provisions for some categories of cost. Second, and crucially, the parameters of price cap regulation must be reset from time to time (e.g. every four or five years). At review points, price cap regulation can become very similar to rate-of-return regulation, and indeed it is well characterised as rate-of-return regulation with long lags.

2.3 *Competition Policy*

Competition policy in regulated industries has three broad aspects - structure, liberalisation, and conduct regulation. Structural policies include break-up decisions such as those taken (or not taken) at the time of privatisation, merger controls, and scope-of-business restrictions. Liberalisation policy is about the removal of legal and economic barriers to entry. Conduct regulation, which may take the form of explicit monopoly controls and/or competition policy measures, constrains the pricing (e.g. of access to natural monopoly networks needed by rival firms) and other behaviour of dominant firms.

Competition policy issues in regulated industries tend to be more complex than those faced by general competition policy for several reasons, including

- dangers that efficient rivals will undesirably be excluded by entry barriers and anti-competitive behaviour by the incumbent monopolist,
- dangers that inefficient rivals will undesirably enter the industry because of distorted price structures inherited from past monopoly (so-called 'cream-skimming'), and
- interactions with regulation (e.g. the use of comparative performance information in price cap design).

Striking a balance between the first and second of these risks has proved particularly problematic in practice.

3   British Experience

3.1   *The Privatisation Programme*

By the time that Mrs Thatcher's Conservative government came to power in 1979, nationalisation by the post-war Labour government and subsequently had led to a situation in which the public sector in Britain dominated the supply of energy (gas, electricity, coal and some oil), transport (air, rail and bus), communications (post and telecommunications) and water, and also had substantial interests in manufacturing (e.g. in aircraft, shipbuilding, steel and cars).

In the eighteen years of Conservative government to 1997, the proportion of British GDP accounted for by state-owned firms fell from 11 per cent to below 2 per cent. At the peak of the privatisation programme, between the mid 1980s and the early 1990s, sales proceeds typically exceeded 1 per cent of GDP and were sometimes of the order of 3 per cent of public expenditure.

The watershed in the British privatisation programme was the sale of British Telecom in 1984, an event which was motivated to a considerable degree by a desire to free BT from macroeconomic restrictions on public sector borrowing. Before that privatisation policies were relatively modest in scale and confined to firms in more or less competitive industries such as oil and manufacturing. By extending the programme to utility monopolies, the sale of BT marked a key shift in the nature, as well as the scale, of the British privatisation programme. In particular, it required the development of a regulatory system.

71

Privatisation - with accompanying regulation - was subsequently extended to gas (1986), airports (1987), water in England and Wales (1989), electricity (1990-91) and the railways (1996). By 1997 the main activities remaining in the public sector were the Post Office, the London Underground, British Nuclear Fuels, Air Traffic Control, and the water industry in Scotland.

The main ways of privatising a firm are (i) offer for sale of shares to the general public, (ii) sale to another firm, and (iii) management/employee buyout. The latter method has been used in parts of the transport sector, including road haulage (National Freight Consortium), some bus companies, and rail rolling stock leasing companies. The Rover car group is an example of privatisation by sale to another firm (British Aerospace, who later sold Rover to BMW). However, by far the most important method used in Britain has been offer for sale to the general public.

With this method, questions include (a) whether to sell the firm in two or more stages, or all at once, (b) whether the share price is set administratively or by competitive tendering among prospective purchasers of the shares, and (c) whether incentives and bonus schemes are created to encourage small investors to buy and hold privatisation shares. Before the BT sale, privatisations were mostly in stages (as was BT's), use was often made of competitive tendering, and no great inducements to wider share ownership were given. These methods are conducive to reasonably accurate share pricing. Thus selling a firm's shares in stages enables accurate pricing after the first stage because the market value of the shares is known.

In the latter part of the 1980s, however, some large firms (e.g. British Gas) were sold in one go, tendering methods were eschewed, and there were strong incentives for small investors to buy and hold shares. This pattern suggests that wider share ownership may have become a primary objective of privatisation policy. In the 1990s tendering methods came back into use, albeit with discounts for small investors, thus combining the objectives of revenue maximisation and wider share ownership to some extent.

Even judged relative to the discounts that are typical with private initial public offerings, the amounts of government revenue forgone in pursuit of the objective of wider share ownership appear to have been very large. The number of British individuals directly owning shares has risen sharply - a process recently strengthened by the demutualisation of building societies - but the proportion of the stock market owned directly by individuals has continued its secular decline. If it is thought to be an appropriate policy goal, wider share ownership might be better pursued by reforms to the taxation of saving and investment generally than as an adjunct to privatisation policies.

3.2 *The Regulatory Framework*

The regulatory framework for the privatised BT was established by the Telecommunications Act 1984. A similar framework has subsequently been adopted for gas, electricity, water and railways. Regulatory powers and duties are divided between the government minister, an industry-specific regulatory body (Oftel in the case of telecommunications) headed by a Director General (DG), and the Monopolies and Mergers Commission (MMC). Regulatory provisions are contained in licences. Licences are granted (or not) by the minister, albeit in consultation with, and sometimes delegation to, the DG. Licences are monitored and enforced by the DG, who may also seek to modify licences either by agreement with licensee or by making a successful reference to the MMC.

For firms with market power, perhaps the most important licence condition is that concerning price control. The British government was anxious to avoid perceived deficiencies of rate-of-return regulation as then practised in the United States. Instead, following the report from Professor Stephen Littlechild (1983), it adopted the form of price cap regulation known as 'RPI-X', which requires an index of the firms regulated prices to fall by X per cent per annum in real terms (i.e. relative to the retail price index) for a period of years. This was intended to be 'regulation with a light rein'. In the event, however, price regulation in several industries became tighter and more detailed over time, and rate-of-return considerations were evidently of prime importance at points of regulatory review. Nevertheless, even if RPI-X price cap regulation is akin to rate-of-return regulation with long lags (for the reasons given above), this may well have substantial advantages over rate-of-return regulation as traditionally practised.

However, RPI-*X* regulation came under heavy criticism around 1995 when share prices in a number of privatised utilities appreciated sharply. These share price gains were partly due to the wave of takeover bids described below. Many argued that 'profit-sharing' - i.e. explicitly linking price inversely to profit - would be fairer than price caps, and that fairness would enhance regulatory credibility and hence investment incentives. But there are arguments against explicit profit sharing. The first is that price caps already implicitly share profits with consumers, albeit with a lag, as prices are adjusted at review points. Second, unless lag is extended (in which case fairness and credibility problems might return), profit-sharing blunts incentives for cost efficiency. Third, profit measurement is prone to problems of subjectivity, circularity (as regards the value of regulated assets) and hence to dispute. Arguably it is better to confront these problems periodically at review points, and to have a simple regulatory contract in the interim, than to face them continuously. Fourth, if (as in practice) there is error in setting the benchmark relative to which excess profit is judged, then profit-sharing need not achieve its aim of enhancing fairness.

3.3 *Competition Policy*

Both BT and British Gas were privatised without restructuring as vertically integrated firms with nationwide dominance. However, after a decade of competition problems arising from the vertical integration of British Gas, and in view of accelerated liberalisation of retail supply, the company divided itself into separate pipeline and supply companies in 1997.

By contrast, the government radically restructured the electricity and railway industries before privatisation. In 1990 the Central Electricity Generating Board (CEGB) in England and Wales was divided into a transmission company (National Grid) and three generators (National Power, PowerGen, and Nuclear Electric, which was eventually privatised in 1996). Vertical separation meant that a new mechanism had to be devised to co-ordinate transmission and generation, and a wholesale auction market, the Pool, was established. Twelve Regional Electricity Companies (RECs) were privatised with responsibility for distribution and retail supply, which has been progressively liberalised.

Restructuring and ownership changes have continued after privatisation. Initially the RECs jointly owned National Grid but it became an independent company in 1995. Most RECs have entered generation in partnership with new entrants. One REC, Eastern, has acquired substantial generation capacity that National Power and PowerGen had to divest following concerns about their market power (which was largely due to the concentrated structure for generation chosen by government in an unsuccessful effort to privatise nuclear power at the outset.)

Takeover threats - in theory an important difference between public and private ownership - became a sharp reality after the lifting of takeover protections in 1995. Most RECs have since been acquired - by water utilities, foreign utilities, and others. However, in 1996 the government vetoed bids for RECs by the generators National Power and PowerGen. Thus, depending on merger policy, industry structure and ownership can alter substantially after privatisation.

British Rail was restructured to form a number of companies, notably Railtrack (network infrastructure, including track and stations) and three rolling stock leasing companies. Its passenger train operations have been privatised by the award of 25 franchises. Public subsidy to rail services continues in the privatised regime.

Statutory monopoly typically accompanied public ownership in the utility industries. Among other things this served to facilitate extensive cross-subsidy - between groups of customers, and sometimes of input suppliers (e.g. the nationalised electricity industry effectively subsidised British Coal). The removal of statutory barriers to entry in telecommunications, gas and electricity began in the early 1980s several years before privatisation policies were adopted. Liberalisation has generally gone further since privatisation, and over time more attention has been given to economic, as well as legal, barriers to entry.

In telecommunications liberalisation of apparatus supply and value-added services began in 1981, when BT was split from the Post Office, and in 1982 Mercury was licensed as a competing network operator. However, for the rest of the decade the government adopted a 'duopoly policy' of allowing no further entry into fixed-link network operation. The rationale for the policy was to promote infrastructure investment by both BT and Mercury and allow time for tariff rebalancing. A parallel duopoly policy applied to mobile telecommunications.

When the duopoly policy was ended in 1991, the interconnection question - on what terms can rivals gain access to BT's network? - was a focus of controversy (as it had been with Mercury earlier). One the one hand it was argued that rivals (e.g. the cable operators now free to offer telecommunications services in their own right) could inefficiently 'cream-skim' BT's more profitable business while BT was hampered by limits on exchange line rental charges, universal service obligations, and regulatory restrictions on the provision of entertainment services over its telecommunications network (the so-called 'broadcasting ban'). On the other hand it was argued that rivals faced entry barriers. These tensions eased somewhat over time as tariff rebalancing diminished cross-subsidies in BT's pricing structure, and as entry barriers (e.g. the lack of number portability) were tackled directly by Oftel.

In conjunction with its review of BT's price regulation from 1997, Oftel introduced into BT's licence, and the licences of other telecommunications operators, a Fair Trading Condition prohibiting anti-competitive behaviour, which is based on Articles 85 and 86 of the Treaty of Rome (unlike UK competition law generally, though this is to be reformed by the new Labour government – see DTI, 1997). At the same time a number of detailed licence conditions were removed and the scope of retail price control was substantially reduced. While less dramatic than the move from nationalisation to regulated private monopoly in 1984, these measures constitute an important shift from monopoly regulation towards competition policy as means of addressing market power in telecommunications.

4 Regulatory Reform in Ireland[4]

4.1 *Public Ownership*

At the time of Telecom Eireann's partial denationalisation in 1996, the scale and pattern of public ownership of industry in Ireland was rather similar to that in Britain in 1979 - with state-owned firms accounting for about 10% of GDP, dominating much of the energy, transport and communications sectors, but also with interests in forestry, fertiliser, health insurance and banking. Privatisation (e.g. of B&I Shipping, Irish Life and Irish Sugar) has been partial and piecemeal, but some steps have been taken to increase the financial and commercial disciplines on state-owned firms.

---

[4] See further OECD, 1993, chapter IV.

Social and political objectives and constraints on state-owned firms nevertheless continue to be of great importance. However, it is important to question whether, and to what extent, public ownership is an efficient way to pursue society's non-economic objectives. And in competitive industries at least, where economic constraints are strong, political constraints are likely to hamper economic efficiency (e.g. efficiency investment) insofar as they are effective. It would seem, then, that there should be a fairly strong presumption in favour of privatising firms in competitive industries, especially if efficient methods of sale (e.g. methods conducive to full prices being achieved by government) are employed.

As regards industries where there is monopoly power, the case of Telecom Eireann is of particular interest. TE was denationalised by strategic alliance: in response to the evident forces of globalisation and consolidation in the industry, the Irish government invited overseas operators to bid for a (minority) stake in TE. A consortium of KPN and Telia, the Dutch and Swedish national telecommunications operators, paid IR£183 million for an initial 20% of TE, with options to buy a further 15% for IR£200 million over the next three years. Further payments will be due under a clawback arrangement according to the growth in TE's share value. This arrangement may go some way towards achieving the fairness objective that has motivated profit sharing proposals in Britain, but without involving price control methods.

4.2 *Regulation*

A Telecommunications Bill was introduced in September 1996 to provide for independent regulation of the industry (in line with EU policy). The Director of Telecommunications Regulation, Etain Doyle, heads an Office of about 50 people — compared with about 160 in Britain's Oftel — funded by charges levied on the industry. Her regulatory powers came into effect on 30 June 1997. A tariff order places a five-year price cap of the RPI-X type on TE, which the regulator will review after two years.

4.3   Competition Policy[5]

The 1991 Competition Act introduced into domestic law prohibitions of anticompetitive agreements between firms and of abuse of dominance in line with Articles 85 and 86 of the Treaty of Rome. The enforcement of these provisions however appears somewhat patchy, though the 1996 Competition (Amendment) Act should sharpen enforcement provided that the authorities are not captured by vested industrial interests.

Before the Amendment Act was passed, private actions were the main vehicle for enforcement, but incentives to bring them are not altogether clear. The Competition Authority established by the 1991 Act has powers of investigation and exemption from the prohibition on anticompetitive agreements; the Amendment Act added public enforcement powers and penalties for breach including criminal sanctions in some cases. The Minister for Enterprise and Employment may bring court actions and, subject to parliamentary approval, may dissolve dominant positions for the common good in some circumstances.

While the basic structure of Irish competition law now appears sound, evident problems remain concerning its implementation. One problem is that major industries - e.g. groceries, transport and telecommunications - effectively enjoy some important exemptions from competition rules. Another is that restrictive licensing policies thwart competition in a number of sectors, including pubs, taxis and pharmacists. Incentives for regulatory capture of licensing policy are powerful. On these matters see further Fingleton, 1997.

Of course Articles 85 and 86 have applied to Irish commerce, insofar as inter-trade is affected, since the country joined the EC. Interesting recent cases, which illustrate the reach of EC competition law, include the *Magill* TV listings cases against RTE and others, *B&I Line v Sealink* concerning the 'essential facility' of Holyhead port, *British Midland v Aer Lingus* concerning interlining on the London-Dublin route, and the Unilever case about freezer exclusivity for 'impulse' ice creams. The Single Market programme, and the forces of globalisation generally, have increased competitive pressure - and enhanced competitive opportunities - for firms supplying tradable goods and services.

---

5   See Fingleton, 1997, for a critique of recent Irish competition policy.

5   EU Liberalisation[6]

Not long ago, 'special sectors' such as energy and telecommunications appeared to enjoy effective exemption from those competitive pressures and from the provisions of EC competition law. In recent years, however, the European Commission, Council and Parliament, through a series of Directives, are requiring Member States to liberalise their public utility industries in certain respects. The key provisions of the Treaty of Rome in this regard are those on free trade in services, and Article 90.

Article 90(1) requires Member States not to enact nor maintain in force any measure contrary to the rules in the Treaty, including the competition rules. Article 90(2) offers some scope for exemption from 90(1) in the case of 'undertakings entrusted with the operation of services of general economic interest or having the character of revenue-producing monopoly' if the application of Treaty rules obstructed their performance of those tasks, provided that trade is not affected against the interests of the Community. Case law has established, however, that competition rules may be disapplied only if there is no other way of performing the tasks in question. Article 90(3) empowers the Commission to enforce Articles 90(1) and 90(2), without needing to go to the Courts or Council of Ministers, by issuing directives to Member States.

5.1   *Telecommunications Liberalisation*

These powers have been used to compel liberalisation of telecommunications. Whereas Britain's relatively early liberalisation means that EU developments (in this area at least) are not a binding constraint on policy, the same is far from true of some other Member States, including Ireland.

The Commission first issued a Directive in 1988 requiring Member States to withdraw exclusive rights over the sale and maintenance of terminal equipment. Two years later liberalisation was extended to some telecommunications services - principally value added and data services, but not voice telephony, telex, mobile communications, paging, satellite, or broadcasting - by Directive 90/388/EEC.

---

[6]   Ungerer, 1996, gives an interesting account of the issues discussed in this section.

Satellite, cable TV networks, and mobile and personal communications were subsequently brought under that Directive. Finally, in March 1996, the Commission issued Directive 96/19/EC requiring full liberalisation of telecommunications - including voice telephony and the provision of telecommunications infrastructure - by 1 January 1998.

The transition period before this date is intended to 'allow telecommunications organisations to complete their preparations for competition and in particular to pursue the necessary rebalancing of tariffs'. Member states with 'less developed networks' (Greece, Ireland, Spain and Portugal) or with 'very small networks' (Luxembourg) were allowed to apply for extensions of the transitional period of up to five and two years respectively, provided that was essential to complete necessary structural adjustments while continuing to meet public service obligations.

5.2 Ireland's Request For Delay

In May 1996 Ireland duly applied for postponements:
- of two years until 1 January 2000 of the ending of TE's monopoly over voice telephony and underlying network infrastructure,
- of three years until 1 July 1999 of the removal of restrictions on liberalised services provided over alternative (i.e. not the incumbent's) infrastructure, and
- until 1 January 2000 of the direct interconnection of mobile networks, which was due in 1996 according to the EC Directive.

The case was made that TE needed the extra time to prepare itself for competition by further developing its network, by rebalancing tariffs, and by restructuring its cost base and service offerings. The main general point was that early liberalisation would deprive TE of revenues (e.g. from international services) necessary for the fulfilment of its public service obligations. Thus it was argued that, as well as TE's exclusive rights over voice telephony and underlying infrastructure monopoly being essential for this purpose, mobile liberalisation would allow bypass of TE's long-distance and international services, and liberalisation of value added services over alternative infrastructure might lead to unofficial bypass of the voice telephony monopoly.

The Irish Congress of Trade Unions supported the government's request for derogation, but other responses were critical. For example, it was argued that TE's network was not so underdeveloped, that mobile liberalisation could generate more rather than less traffic for TE, that unofficial bypass of voice telephony could be stopped, that delay would serve to entrench TE's dominance, and that competition could benefit rather than harm public service objectives. Furthermore, the effects of eventual liberalisation, especially in the local loop, might be weakened by TE's majority ownership of the main cable TV operator Cablelink (a situation that contrasts strongly with that in Britain).

Subject to conditions, the European Commission decided to allow the requested voice telephony postponement until 2000, to allow mobile interconnection liberalisation to be delayed only until 1999 (a year earlier than requested), but to require liberalisation of services over alternative infrastructure from mid-1997 (two years earlier than requested). The conditions related inter alia to the timetable for liberalising legislation and licensing, and a requirement that Cablelink be run at arm's length from TE.

On voice telephony it was judged that the negative impact on trade was limited because of the relatively small scale of the Irish market, the two-year limit of the proposed derogation, and other factors including TE's not planning to expand abroad. On mobile it was decided that liberalisation might put at risk the financing of TE's public service obligations out of international traffic, and that the negative effect on trade might be limited especially if TE gave volume discounts to mobile operators. However, on liberalised services over alternative infrastructure, the Commission decided that monopoly was unnecessary to stop bypass of voice telephony at least once the independent regulatory authority was in place.

On the face of it the Commission (and indeed the Irish Government) were generous to the beneficiaries - notably TE - of the request for delayed liberalisation. If a two year extension of monopoly in Ireland does limited harm, why is the same not true of other Member States? Why should the application of single market competition rules be related to country size? How is it known by public officials that large players would not want to invest rapidly in Ireland? Why should a monopoly that chooses not to export have more protection from import competition than one that engages in trade? More generally, why is monopoly necessary for the financing of public service obligations? Why not finance them from interconnection charges or, better, from general taxation or at least an industry-wide levy that is competitively neutral?

6   Conclusions

It is said that an economist should refrain from commenting on policy in a country other than his own unless he has direct experience of its conditions at least to the extent of having flown through its airspace during daylight hours. Happily I pass this test with landing colours in the case of Ireland, but the following ten suggested lessons from Britain are offered tentatively.

(a) For firms in competitive industries, privatisation is generally good for economic efficiency. Ireland should consider early privatisation of its public enterprises in those industries, which are subject to competition (including airline and financial services sectors). This would include Aer Lingus, ACCBank, Trustee Savings Bank and the Industrial Credit Corporation.

(b) It is best to use privatisation sales methods that ensure that the extent of underpricing is no more than modest (except perhaps in the case of employees of the firms in question). Large underpricing has fiscal and distributional costs, and may give rise to a sense of unfairness that may weaken policy credibility.

(c) For firms with market power, it is hard to isolate the effects of privatisation from those of regulatory and competitive reforms. Focus on those irrespective of ownership, and implement them before privatisation (if that is to happen) for the sake of regulatory stability ex post, which is crucial for investment incentives.

(d) The keys to successful regulatory reform are adherence to the maxim 'competition where possible, regulation where necessary', and independent economic regulation.

(e) Price cap regulation, though a form of rate-of-return regulation with long lags, provides a price control framework with better incentive properties than rate-of-return regulation as traditionally practised, and is also superior to explicit profit-sharing schemes.

82

(f) Competition policy applies to structure, liberalisation, and conduct. Structural 'ring-fencing' (i.e. separate ownership) of natural monopoly elements is desirable unless scope economies are large. Such restructuring should happen before any privatisation. In regulated industries merger policy should take account of ways in which mergers can weaken regulation (e.g. by losing comparative performance information) as well as possible anti-competitive effects.

(g) There should be a strong presumption in favour of open liberalisation policies – i.e. free entry. Where entry slots are finite (e.g. because of spectrum scarcity), both fiscal and efficiency considerations favour the use of auction methods provided that the auctions would be reasonably competitive.

(h) Significantly anti-competitive agreements and abuses of market power should be subject to prohibitions backed by penalties and scope for action for damages by third parties. Articles 85 and 86 of the Treaty of Rome provide a reasonably good framework for this purpose (even though some EC case law is open to question). The prohibitions should apply as generally as possible, subject of course to efficiency defences (such as that in Article 85(3)), and not be blunted by various exemptions and exclusions for 'special cases'.

(i) In particular, there should be scepticism about disapplying competition rules for the sake of public service obligations or the protection of cross-subsidies. This is not because public service obligations, or even cross-subsidies, are bad, but because monopoly is usually an inferior way of financing them. Explicit taxes and subsidies are generally to be preferred to hidden ones.

(j) The political challenge of ensuring that vested interests in the status quo do not capture the process of reform to the detriment of the many is not to be underestimated. Ireland's obligations under EU directives might be helpful in this regard, depending on the rigour of their application and, above all perhaps, the future direction of EU policy in this sphere.

References

Armstrong, M., S. Cowan and J. Vickers, 1994, *Regulatory Reform*, MIT Press, Cambridge MA.

Boardman, A. and A.R. Vining, 1989, "Ownership and Performance in Competitive Environments: A Comparison of the Performance of Private, Mixed, and State-Owned Enterprises", *Journal of Law and Economics*, 32, pp. 1-33.

Fingleton, J., 1997, "Standards of Competition in the Irish Economy", *Journal of the Statistical and Social Inquiry Society of Ireland*, forthcoming.

Galal, A., L. Jones, P. Tandon and I. Vogelsang, 1994, *Welfare Consequences of Selling Public Enterprises: An Empirical Analysis*, Oxford University Press, Oxford.

Hart, O., 1995, *Firms, Contracts, and Financial Structure*, Clarendon Press, Oxford.

Littlechild, S.C., 1983, *Regulation of British Telecommunications Profitability*, HMSO, London.

Megginson, W.L., R.C. Nash, and M. van Randenborgh, 1994, "The Financial and Operating Performance of Newly Privatized Firms: An International Empirical Analysis", *Journal of Finance*, 49, pp. 403-452.

OECD, 1993.

Schmidt, K.M., 1996, "The Costs and Benefits of Privatization: An Incomplete Contracts Approach", *Journal of Law, Economics and Organization*, 12, pp. 1-24.

Shapiro, C. and R.D. Willig, "Economic Rationales for the Scope of Privatisation", in E.N. Suleiman and J. Waterbury, editors, *The Political Economy of Public Sector Reform and Privatization*, Westview Press, Boulder CO.

Ungerer, H., 1996, "EU Perspective on Telecommunications Liberalization", paper given at IBEC/B&F conference, Dublin, September.

Vickers, J. and G. Yarrow, 1988, *Privatization: An Economic Analysis*, MIT Press, Cambridge MA.

Vickers, J., 1997, "Privatization", in P. Newman, editor, *The New Palgrave Dictionary of Economics and the Law*, Macmillan, forthcoming.

Persistently High Irish Unemployment: A Comparison with the UK

Michael C. Burda*

Humboldt-Universität zu Berlin and CEPR

1   Introduction

Economics has little hope of achieving the status of a hard science like physics, chemistry or biology for the simple reason that our world - populated as it is by human beings - does not permit laboratory experiments. Although experimental economic research remains a growth industry, in the end the live subjects are usually students (because they are cheap) with little real world experience, and the credibility of the results are haunted by the Hawthorne effect - that people seem to behave differently in experimental situations. Thus whenever nature provides us with a clean, identifiable break of an economic system with the past or with its own environment, economists see attributes of a controlled experiment. 'Event studies' can thus become the subject of intense research interest, as the transformation of central and eastern Europe, German unification, and European Monetary Union illustrate.

When asked to examine Ireland's labour market performance over the past two decades, I immediately saw the makings of such a study. As a graduate student in the early 1980s, and as the son of a Liverpudlian mum with both English and Irish ancestors, I was interested in the marked difference in policies in Ireland and Britain. Although Ireland had different initial conditions (a much larger agricultural sector for starters), both countries managed OPEC I and II badly and had severe structural problems at the outset of the 1980s.

*I am grateful to Alan W. Gray for help with data, Barbara Dluhosch, Alan W. Gray and Stefan Profit for helpful comments and suggestions, Stefan Profit for excellent research assistance and to the Deutsche Forschungsgemeinschaft for resources.

This paper has the modest goal of looking back over the past two decades and comparing these two 'Anglo-Celtic' entities, which share more culture, tradition and weather than they care to admit. The fundamental difference in economic policy between Ireland and Britain is that the former did not experience the Great Regime Change of 1979. In contrast to the UK's policy of tax-cutting, privatisation, and confrontation with trade unions, Ireland opted for a "continental" solution of "high taxes, generous welfare provision; a top-down industrial strategy; and an incomes policy in the form of social contracts signed by government, trade unions and employers".[1] Could this explain its current labour market malaise? The objective of my contribution is to explore this hypothesis.[2]

2   A Parting of the Ways: Ireland's Persistent Unemployment

2.1 Diverging Equilibrium Rates of Unemployment

Either in relative or absolute terms, recent growth performance of the Irish economy - about 5% per annum since 1990 - has been outstanding, and the business and financial press has taken every available opportunity to marvel at "Europe's Shining Light" (*Economist* May 17, 1997) and the new "economic miracle" (*Financial Times*, July 30, 1997). Nevertheless, the Emerald Tiger has been less than outstanding in its ability to share its miracle with the most disadvantaged participants in the labour market. While GDP per person on a purchasing power basis now approaches that of Britain, the jobless rate (ILO-definition) remains stubbornly high at more than 12% in 1996, or nearly twice that in the United Kingdom. As the last panel of figure 1 shows, the differential unemployment rate between the two countries, after having narrowed for decades and reaching an all-time low in 1980, rose dramatically in the 1980s and persists at a higher level today, despite higher economic growth in Ireland. Figure 2 shows that the inflation rate has stabilised in tandem in both countries. These two facts - divergence of average unemployment rates over the cycle plus a stabilisation of inflation rates - are evidence that a fundamental shift has occurred in the equilibrium rates of unemployment in the two countries. That is to say, the unemployment rate consistent with stable nominal wage and price growth has changed in one country or the other, or both.[3]

---

[1] *The Economist,* May 17 1997, p. 24

[2] As an 'event study' this paper will therefore avoid the construction, estimation and simulation of econometric models, as in Newell and Symons, 1990 and Barry and Bradley, 1991.

[3] A more detailed discussion of alternative definitions of the NAIRU or equilibrium unemployment rate as well as procedures used to estimate them can be found in Staiger et al,1997.

Figure 1 Unemployment in Ireland and the United Kingdom

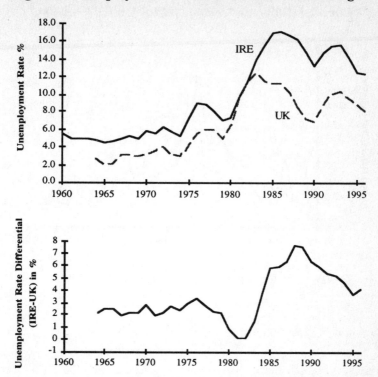

Source: Ireland : *OECD Economic Outlook*, 1960-1982, standardised unemployment rates, *OECD Quarterly Labour Force Statistics*, 1983-1997:2; United Kingdom: standardised unemployment rates, *OECD Main Economic Indicators*, 1964 - 1997:2.

Another way of summarising figure 1 is that while both countries have exhibited a typical European pattern of secularly rising joblessness, Britain has done a superior job in reversing this trend over the past fifteen years, by almost all accounts reducing its equilibrium rate of unemployment. This relatively unheralded achievement - which is undeniably attributable to supply-side reforms in the 1980s - will be examined more closely in this essay. A central question will be in what sense the Irish rejected this approach; more importantly, to what extent this rejection and Ireland's 'continental leanings' are to blame for the labour market blemish on Ireland's otherwise outstanding economic report card.[4]

---

[4] My essay is very much in the spirit of Ashenfelter and Card (1986), who studied the divergence of unemployment rates between the US and Canada in the late 1970s and early 1980s.

Figure 2 Inflation in Ireland and the United Kingdom

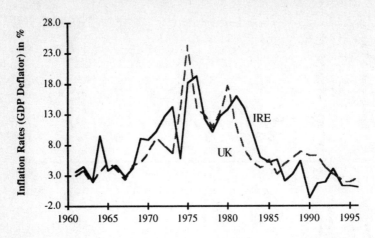

Source: OECD Main Economic Indicators, 1961 - 1997:2.

2.2 *Divergence Despite Integration*

The divergence of labour market performance in Ireland and the UK is somewhat puzzling given the extensive economic integration between the two countries. Basic economics teaches us that integrated economics tend to have similar economic fortunes, at least under idealised conditions. This type of integration can be achieved by a variety of mechanisms.

Most importantly, international trade integrates economies. Nations which trade together tend to have closely-linked goods prices, and under general conditions convergent goods prices tend to induce convergent factor prices (i.e. wages and profit rates); this is the famous factor price equalisation theorem. In the Irish-British case, OECD bilateral trade statistics displayed in table 1 confirm that trade tightly links Britain and Ireland: in 1994 36% and 24% of Irish imports and exports involved the UK directly, while 3.8% and 5.2% of the UK's imports and exports were with Ireland, which is enormous given Ireland's size.[5] While much of this trade is in agricultural products, this share has given way in recent years to non-traditional sectors (Walsh 1996).

---

[5] France and Italy have populations 16.5 times larger than Ireland's, the Netherlands is 4.3 times larger, Belgium and Luxembourg 3.5 times larger.

Table 1 Irish and British Trade Patterns, 1994 (in millions of US dollars)

Ireland	Import	%	Export	%	Total Volume	%
TOTAL	25,686		34,071		59,757	
Trade With						
1. United Kingdom	9,324	36.3	8,203	24.1	17,527	29.3
2. United States	4,701	18.3	2,852	8.4	7,553	12.6
3. Germany	1,814	7.1	4,805	14.1	6,619	11.1
4. France	980	3.8	3,128	9.2	4,108	6.9
5. Netherlands	722	2.8	1,884	5.5	2,606	4.4
6. Japan	1,232	4.8	1,072	3.1	2,304	3.9
7. Italy	568	2.2	1,317	3.9	1,885	3.2
8 Spain	858	3.3	828	2.4	1,686	2.8
9. Belgium/Luxembourg	343	1.3	1,331	3.9	1,674	2.8
10. Sweden	370	1.4	755	2.2	1,125	1.9

UK	Import	%	Export	%	Total Volume	%
TOTAL	230,728		202,152		432,880	
Trade with						
1. Germany	32,701	14.2	24,523	12.1	57,224	13.2
2. United States	25,735	11.2	23,177	11.5	48,912	11.3
3. France	21,876	9.5	19,554	9.7	41,430	9.6
4. Netherlands	14,639	6.3	13,950	6.9	28,589	6.6
5. Belgium/Luxembourg	10,071	4.4	10,961	5.4	21,032	4.9
6. Italy	11,319	4.9	9,651	4.8	20,970	4.8
7. Ireland	8,711	3.8	10,581	5.2	19,292	4.5
8. Japan	13,710	5.9	4,401	2.2	18,111	4.2
9. Spain	5,568	2.4	7,451	3.7	13,019	3.0
10. Sweden	5,890	2.6	4,729	2.3	10,619	2.5

Source: OECD Trade Statistics

One consequence of trade integration has been convergence of hourly wages for manufacturing workers. According to the US Bureau of Labour Statistics, which computes detailed international productivity and labour cost comparisons, average hourly compensation costs in 1995 were for all practical purposes identical: $13.77 in the UK compared with $13.83 in Ireland. In comparison, in 1985 these figures were $6.27 and $5.92 respectively. It should be further noted that factor price convergence result can extend to wages in nontraded goods as well. As long as sectoral productivity is comparable between two countries and workers are mobile between traded and non traded sectors within a country, convergent product prices imply that wage levels cannot deviate too far from one another.

Second, capital mobility also works to enforce convergence of wages and labour market conditions. For its size, Ireland has one of the largest negative investment positions in the world; in 1993, GDP exceeds GNP by almost 12%, and most of this difference was repatriated income earned by foreign-owned capital. According to most accounts, it has been the introduction of new techniques and processes, and not the modernisation of existing operations, which are responsible for Ireland's boom of late. These are almost exclusively attributable to foreign firms, which, according to the *Economist* article, account for 30% of economic activity and 40% of exports. To the extent that Irish workers are employed because they are cheaper than elsewhere, raising the demand for their labour will tend to raise wages as well as reduce unemployment rates.

Finally, labour mobility, for which Ireland is particularly noteworthy, will also equalise wages and labour market conditions.[6] Between Ireland and the UK this linkage is of enormous significance. According to OECD and Irish Census statistics, roughly 220,000 Irish nationals were legally resident in the UK in 1993, representing almost a quarter of all resident aliens in Britain (and fully 6% of the Irish domestic population stock!). The migration flow to the UK continues to amount to 50-60% of annual flows from Ireland.[7] The effect of all this mobility by Irishmen (and women) is to equalise the utility level of residence for the marginal migrant. This includes both the wage as well as the probability of obtaining a job, for which the unemployment rate can be taken as a crude indicator.

---

[6] Ireland has lost a large chunk of its population over the past 150 years. In 1841, the population of the geographic region comprising the Republic of Ireland was over 6.5 million; by the beginning of the century it had declined to 3.25 million; it reached its nadir in 1961 of 2.8 million (OECD 1995).

[7] OECD, 1995, and Central Statistics Office, Dublin.

Persistently high unemployment in Ireland is particularly puzzling when one considers that the Irish economic boom has been accompanied by strong employment growth, as table 2 shows. This growth has been especially pronounced in services and has occurred despite a dramatic decline in agriculture. It remains a central mystery that Ireland continues to have very high unemployment rates despite a sustained expansion of output and employment.

Table 2 Total Civilian Employment Growth in % Per Annum, 1975-1994

	1975-1979	1980-1984	1985-1989	1990-1994
Ireland				
Total	1.3	-0.9	0.3	1.6
Agriculture	-1.5	-2.7	-0.6	-2.8
Industry	1.6	-3.0	0.0	0.9
Services	2.2	1.0	0.7	3.0
UK				
Total	0.3	-0.9	1.7	-0.8
Agriculture	-0.6	-1.2	-1.7	-1.2
Industry	-0.6	-3.9	0.2	-1.5
Services	0.9	0.9	2.5	-0.5

Source: OECD Annual Labour Force Statistics

In my view, there are two competing explanations. Among others, Walsh, 1992, has adduced the interesting hypothesis that migration flows render labour supply in Ireland more elastic than in other economies. In this view, procyclical fluctuations in the labour force induced by expatriates willing to work are responsible for Irish unemployment being 'stuck' at current high levels. According to the argument, the willingness to work - and therefore the involuntary nature of Irish unemployment - can be called into question.

The competing hypothesis is that Ireland has a very large 'discouraged worker' pool, much like the migrants in Walsh's account. The labour force has been reduced over the past three decades by disastrous employment prospects; this "mass of discouragement" consists both of people from rural households as well as unskilled urban workers, and includes women whose participation in other countries skyrocketed in the 1970s and 1980s. This phenomenon has its roots in a secular yet dramatic contraction in agriculture over the past three decades documented in table 5. The fraction of individuals in farming, fishing and forestry has declined from 24% to 13% of the total civilian employment in the past quarter century alone (OECD, 1996). Attached to the large remaining agricultural workforce are family members who work without pay, especially spouses.

I have investigated this issue in two crude ways. First, if true, the first hypothesis implies that unemployment rates for the young in Ireland would tend to exhibit less fluctuation than for older demographic groups. This is because the young are most mobile and adaptable and tend to respond to small changes in migration incentives. Small perturbations in their employment prospects will be met by in- or out-migration.[8] I calculated coefficients of variation of unemployment for seven age groups for both genders for the period 1973 - 1995; the results are presented in table 3. Two results are noteworthy. First, the variability of youth unemployment rates in Ireland is markedly lower than in Britain. Second, variability increases with age more sharply in Ireland than in Britain, although in the later age groups the coefficients of variation are virtually identical. While the results support the migration equilibrium hypothesis, they could be consistent with the hypothesis that domestic labour supply is relatively elastic for younger age groups, especially if it is associated with some form of industrial, occupational, or regional mobility.

---

[8] For a more rigorous implementation of this idea, see Topel, 1986.

Table 3 Variability of Unemployment Rates by Demographic Group

| | Coefficient of Variation of Unemployment Rate | | | |
| | Ireland | | UK | |
For Age Group	Male	Female	Male	Female
15-19[1]	0.10	0.08	0.20	0.24
20-24	0.14	0.14	0.21	0.20
25-34	0.14	0.17	0.18	0.26
35-44	0.12	0.32	0.21	0.17
45-54	0.15	0.24	0.17	0.16
55-64	0.23	0.12	0.13	0.20
65+	0.35	0.38	0.35	0.35

[1] for UK : 16-19

Source: OECD Labour Force Statistics, author's calculations

Second, I use the labour force identity to 'decompose' measured employment changes into changes in unemployment and labour force, and compare these with in-migration flows over the same period.[9] Table 4 shows how this identity evolves for England and Ireland over four five-year intervals, where for convenience all variables are measured relative to total resident working age population at the beginning of the period. The results do not particularly support the hypothesis that employment and labour force changes are driven by migration movements, but rather seem orthogonal to them.[10] Apparently the often-described 'migration equilibrium' between Ireland and its host countries may have broken down in recent years (see also Honohan, 1992). Naturally, it is *relative* prospects which determine migration flows, so the UK recession in the early 1990s may have dampened the attractiveness of migration to Irish young people (Walsh, 1992).

---

[9] Formally, $\Delta e = -\Delta u + \Delta n$ where e, u, n stand respectively for employment, unemployment, and labour force.

[10] After examining correlation coefficients for both log levels as well as first differences in the logs of annual series, as well as at one and two lags, it is evident that the linkage between migration and employment growth is by no means a simple bivariate one.

Table 4 Sources of Employment Growth 1975-1994
(In % of resident working age population)

	1975-1979	1980-1984	1985-1989	1990-1994
Ireland				
Total change in employment	4.0	-2.7	1.2	3.1
= total change in labour force	4.2	3.0	-0.3	4.3
- total change in unemployment	-0.2	-5.7	1.5	-1.2
memo: total net out-migration	-2.8	2.1	7.4	1.4
UK				
Total change in employment	1.4	-2.3	6.1	-4.2
= total change in labour force	1.8	1.9	2.6	-1.8
- total change in unemployment	-0.4	-4.1	3.5	-2.4
memo: total net out-migration	0.2	0.3	-0.6	-1.1[1]

[1] 1990-1993 only

While not ruling out a potential contribution for migration (especially for skilled workers), it seems more plausible that internal labour force movements (from the underground economy or the state of discouragement) are primarily responsible for recent movements in employment, especially in the last decade. Some general evidence for this can be found in the panels of figure 3, which compares employment rates (total employment divided by working age population, OECD), labour force participation rates (employment plus unemployment divided by the working-age population) as well as migration rates for the two countries. Despite robust employment growth documented earlier, the *employment rate* in Ireland - a better measure of labour market performance than the unemployment rate, as it is not distorted by the participation decision - is abysmally low.[11]

Poor employment performance has coincided with very low rates of labour force participation compared with other OECD countries. The difference is most striking for women: in 1995 female participation was 47.6% of the working age population, compared with 65.4% in the UK (the OECD average was roughly 60%). Unlike most European countries, overall labour force participation

---

[11] The employment rate is defined as the ratio of total employment to the working age population; the nonemployment rate is 1 minus the employment rate. Both of these concepts are relatively immune to labour force participation patterns.

declined in Ireland over the past three decades. At the same time the existence of a large backwash of expatriate labour does not suggest that the local population is unconditionally willing to work at current conditions on offer - one has to explain why the locals weren't taken first. Yet the fact that employment and migration are uncorrelated over long periods suggests that the expatriate population is not central to explaining why unemployment remains so stubbornly high in Ireland. Part of the problem seems to be that there are simply not enough jobs to employ an already lean labour force.

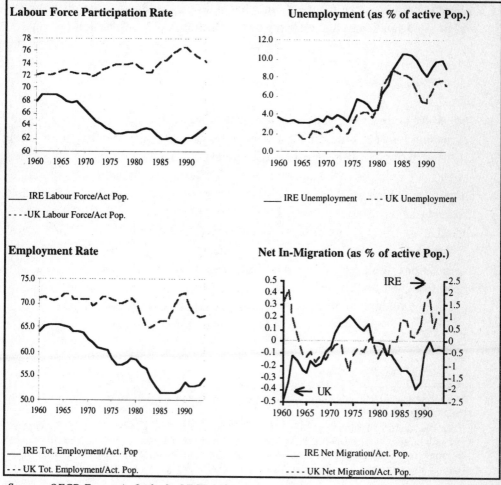

Figure 3 Comparative Labour Market Indicators in Ireland and the UK

Source: OECD Economic Outlook; OECD Labour Force Survey.

3   The Usual Suspects

Some economists, including Dornbusch, 1989, have criticised the Irish stabilisation in the 1980s for inducing a sharp rise in unemployment and some continue to blame tight fiscal policy for Ireland's woes. Yet most economists tend not to consider demand movements as causing longer term movement of the equilibrium rate, so this cannot explain the rise in Irish joblessness relative to the UK.[12] Rather it would seem logical to turn to Ireland's structural problems. Some candidates are related to Ireland's particularly dominant agricultural heritage and its modest degree of industrialisation, its system of collective bargaining, regulation of the labour market, unemployment benefits, social minima, and excessive taxation. In what follows, I address some of the most widely cited candidates and offer my own reflections on their plausibility.

3.1 *Collective Bargaining*

One widely-cited explanation of upwardly ratcheting unemployment rates in continental Europe is the role of collective bargaining. In particular, unions and other institutions tend to represent the interests of 'insiders' (job-holders) at the expense of outsiders (the unemployed). Differing institutions of collective bargaining, which are central to this explanation, might therefore account for diverging labour market performance.[13] Traditionally, Ireland and Britain have shared a number of institutions in collective bargaining; labour unions are organised along crafts lines, and are weakly associated in large umbrella organisations (the Irish Congress of Trade Unions or ICTU in Ireland, the Trade Union Congress or TUC in the UK). As in Britain, wage negotiation in Ireland is a system of voluntary collective bargaining at either local or national level.

---

[12] In recent years some economists have begun to question the utility of this concept. See for example Galbraith, 1997.

[13] See Blanchard and Summers, 1986 for the first statement of this idea. A related hypothesis adduced by Calmfors and Driffill, 1988 is that either extreme centralisation or decentralisation of bargaining encourages wage moderation in collective bargaining, whereas intermediate union structures are associated with wage demands inconsistent with high employment.

Over the past fifteen years, however, a divergence of the two systems of collective bargaining has become evident. In the UK, the government has actively encouraged decentralisation of wage fixing mechanisms and the introduction of flexible pay arrangements matching enterprise performance and local labour market conditions, and the 1990s have seen a steady shift from collective wage fixing to individual agreements. Employers have received tax relief for introducing profit-related pay schemes. Early in the 1980s, the government instituted sweeping reforms of labour law, eliminating the excesses of the closed shop and allowing more democracy in union leadership choice and decision making. The only obvious intervention of government into the pay-setting process is an ongoing limit on nominal pay increases on the public sector, limiting wage growth to improvements of efficiency.

In contrast, Ireland has taken an explicitly more corporatist approach to collective bargaining. Although Irish unions lost almost a quarter of their members in the 1980s, union density remains higher than in the UK (roughly 55% in 1990 compared to the low 40s in Britain). In response, Irish unions have sought to consolidate organisational structures and worker advocacy into larger industrial unions. Since 1988, Irish trade unions have concluded nationwide, centralised pay agreements in explicit tripartite negotiations with government and employers' associations, with the explicit goal of moderating wage growth, often in exchange for tax relief. The Programme for Competitiveness and Work covered the period 1994-6 and anticipated 8% total wage growth over the years 1994-6. This was followed by the 1996 Partnership 2000 agreement which has similar objectives.

While 'insider power' is sometimes cited as causing ever-increasing unemployment rates in Ireland, the recent behaviour of insiders in Ireland seems to belie the hypothesis. The insider-outsider view would have predicted strong real wage hikes in recent years in response to robust economic growth - as was observed in the UK in the late 1980s, and not the remarkable wage moderation observed in Ireland over the past five years.

3.2 *Severance Regulations*

Irish unemployment seems more persistent than Britain's - shocks lasted longer in Ireland, whereas fluctuations themselves are larger in Britain. One plausible explanation for this is that job protection regulations - including firing costs, severance benefits and administrative red-tape - induce employers to hire more cautiously in upturns and to fire less frequently in downturns.

Table 5 displays the state of play in 1996, Ireland has long rejected the extreme notion of hire-at-will in the US, yet has not gone much further than Britain in offering 'protection' to its workers. In the area of economic (mass) redundancies, which is of the greatest importance for job creation, there seems to be little substantive difference with the UK which is well-recognised as the most liberal regime concerning severance law in Europe. It would appear then that this factor is not responsible for Ireland's unemployment problem.

Table 5 Regulation of Redundancy in Ireland and Britain

Type of Redundancy	Ireland	United Kingdom
Individual:		
Required Period of Notice	One week after 13 weeks' service up to 8 weeks after 15 years' service or more	None
Redundancy Pay/Severance Benefit	Average redundancy pay: 10 weeks pay	Guaranteed by law, depends on age, pay and length of service and provisions in the employment contract
Collective (mass):		
Definition	If a firm of size n makes m workers redundant over 30 days and: $m \geq 5$ for $20 < n < 50$ $m \geq 10$ for $50 < n < 100$ $m \geq 10$ for $100 < n < 300$ $m \geq 30$ for $n > 300$	If a firm dismisses at least 20 employees at one establishment within 90 days for reasons not related to individual
Required Period of Notice	1 - 8 weeks' notice or compensation and according to agreement	1 - 12 weeks' notice or pay
Redundancy Pay/Severance Benefit	Guaranteed by law, depends on length of service and age	Guaranteed by law, depends on length of service and employment contract
Consultation	Workforce delegates, Department of Enterprise and Employment to be notified	Either recognised trade unions or elected representatives of the individual concerned

Source: European Commission, 1997

Another frequently-cited cause of persistent unemployment is the social safety net, in particular unemployment benefits. As the argument has it, labour market performance is adversely affected by benefit systems that offer too much income replacement after tax, are paid out for too long durations or cast too wide a net. First, workers' choosiness may rise, leading to a lower frequency of job acceptance at a given wage offer. Second, by raising the 'fall back' position of trade unions, generous unemployment benefits tilt the bargaining table in favour of labour. Third, by increasing the workers' wage expectations in general, the benefit levels can suppress low-pay jobs corresponding to low productivity occupations and industries simply because no one would accept them.

The system of unemployed benefits in Ireland - Pay Related Social Insurance Scheme (PRSI) - offers benefit to the unemployed for 390 days at full rate, which is graduated according to previous earnings with a cap.[14] After benefits expire, workers have a means-tested claim on unemployment assistance, which is open-ended, meaning that there is no statutory time limitation on benefit receipt. The OECD estimates the after tax replacement rate for a couple with no children is 49% in Ireland compared with 35% in Britain. There is also a Part-time Job Incentive Scheme which pays the unemployed £42.70 per week (£70.30 if there is an additional adult in the house, which can be claimed when the worker in question has a part-time job).

In the United Kingdom, unemployment benefit is paid at a flat-rate per week for 182 days (which was reduced from 1 year in 1996). Anyone who works less than sixteen hours per week is eligible. As in Ireland, unemployment assistance in the UK is open-ended, but it is suspected that the means test and especially the work test are applied more rigorously there than in Ireland. Indeed a much larger fraction of Irish GDP is paid out to recipients of unemployment benefit than the UK, but this fraction has been falling over time as workers have lost their eligibility.[15] Only in 1995 was the separate earnings-related benefit abolished, which is comparable to the system that was eliminated in Britain in 1983.

---

[14] According to the brochure "Social Welfare Rates of Payment 1997/98" (Department of Social Welfare), a maximal flat rate of £67.50 per week is payable to each registered unemployed person, plus £40.00 per week for each qualified adult plus £13.20 for each child dependant (which may be reduced if there is no second adult in the household!). For earnings less than £70/week, rates are reduced accordingly. Unemployment assistance is almost identical to unemployment benefit levels.

[15] The OECD *Economic Outlook* reports that in the last year reported, 1991, Ireland spent 3.25% of GDP on passive measures (unemployment benefits and early retirement for labour market reasons), and 1.48% on active labour market policies; while Britain spent 1.41% of GDP on passive measures and 0.57% on active measures (OECD 1996).

An important side-effect of generous provision of unemployment benefit and especially social assistance is the suppression of labour supply to low-pay jobs. For all their bad press, low-pay jobs provide a means of social and economic integration for those whose skills are in relatively low demand. In Anglo-Saxon economies they have provided an important - although not exclusive - source of employment growth for displaced workers. Recent policy initiatives, especially in the US and Britain, have begun to employ the tax system to alleviate the inequality associated with these jobs, while keeping people in work.[16] Many of these low-pay jobs are in the services: trade, eating and drinking establishments, hotels, personal and business services. The last column of table 6 shows that, despite impressive growth in Ireland and despite the severe recession in the UK, Irish workers in broadly defined services as a fraction of the working age population (18.3%) remains modest compared to Britain (26.2%).

It is therefore instructive to look at measures of the dispersion of pay in both countries. Since I am interested in low wages as a stimulus to job creation rather than as the source of inequality, it seemed more appropriate to review data on sectoral inequality. To this end I display a crude measure of the dispersion of annual compensation wages across approximate 1-digit sectors. My data source is the OECD National Accounts, which report relatively crude breakdowns of total wages and salaries paid at the sectoral level. I divided these by salaried employees in corresponding sectoral groupings to obtain seven series for annual employee compensation dating back to 1975. In figure 4 the evolution of coefficients of variation of these compensation measures across the sectors is reported for the two countries, where the values are normalised to unity in 1975 correct for measurement error in the absolute levels.[17]

The figure supports two conclusions. First, Britain experienced a dramatic increase in sectoral pay inequality during the Thatcher regime, which was primarily due to the sharp increase in salaries in the financial sector and the decline in poorly paid services and retail. Second, and surprisingly, is the conclusion that this inequality declined sharply in the years subsequent to 1987

---

[16] For a discussion of these issues, see Nickell, 1996.

[17] The coefficient of variation is the sample standard deviation divided by the sample mean. In constructing these measures I weight by the relative size of the sector using employment shares.

by some measures to the levels at the beginning of the sample. The pay inequality often noted as a by-product of the past two decades (Nickell 1996) seems to be a result of inequality within, and not between sectors. It would be patently false to dismiss British employment growth as the impoverished employment of fast food workers and shop clerks.

Table 6 Growth in Salaried Employment in %, five year intervals 1975-1994

Ireland	1975-1979	1980-1984	1985-1989	1990-1994	*Memo:* 1994 level as % of working-age population
Total	6.7	-4.6	2.3	5.6	54.1
Agriculture	-7.1	-12.9	-3.0	-13.2	6.5
Manufacturing	6.7	-14.4	4.9	7.3	10.6
Electr. gas & water	0.0	7.1	-6.7	7.7	0.6
Construction	13.5	-17.5	-7.7	0.0	3.5
Wholesale/retail trade, restaurants & hotels	6.8	0.0	0.5	21.1	10.5
Transport, storage & communication	-1.5	-1.4	-2.9	7.4	3.3
Financial insurance, real estate & business services	37.2	18.5	11.7	11.0	4.5
Community, social and personal services	13.3	9.1	7.0	16.2	14.1
UK	**1975-1979**	**1980-1984**	**1985-1989**	**1990-1994**	***Memo:* 1994 level as % of working-age population**
Total	2.0	-3.2	9.2	-5.9	67.7
Agriculture	-3.1	-5.8	3.7	-6.8	1.4
Manufacturing	-3.4	-17.2	0.7	-16.9	13.0
Electr. gas & water	-1.7	102.8	-16.2	-37.8	1.0
Construction	-1.7	13.3	17.9	-12.9	4.9
Wholesale/retail trade, restaurants & hotels	4.7	0.3	11.6	-4.7	13.7
Transport, storage & communication	-1.0	-7.2	14.8	-3.7	4.2
Financial insurance, real estate & business services	8.9	9.5	27.9	2.3	8.3
Community, social and personal services	5.3	-6.1	9.1	7.9	20.8

Source: OECD Economic Outlook : total employment.

Figure 4 Relative Sectoral Wage Dispersion in Ireland and the UK, 1975-93
(1975=1.0)

a) All Sectors [1]

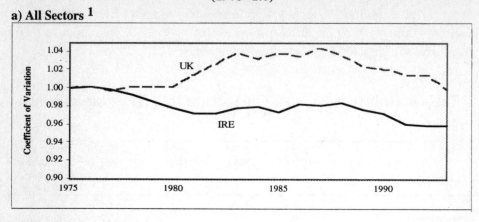

b) Excluding Agriculture

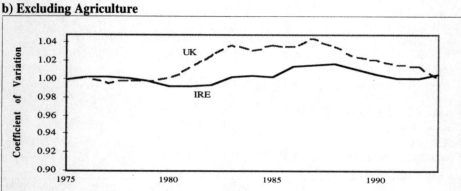

c) Excluding Industry

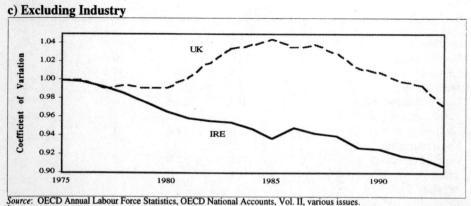

Source: OECD Annual Labour Force Statistics, OECD National Accounts, Vol. II, various issues.

[1] Compensation per employee in Ireland and UK for the following sectors: (a) agriculture, hunting, forestry and fishing, (b) construction, (c) wholesale, retail trade, restaurants and hotels, (d) transport, storage and communication, (e) finance, insurance, real estate, business services, (f) community, social and personal services, and (g) other industries (mining and quarrying, manufacturing, electricity, gas and water) for both countries.

4 The Great Regime Change in the UK and the Fiscal-Unemployment Trap in Ireland

4.1 *A Tale of Two Fiscal Policies*

What Margaret Thatcher accomplished during her twelve years of office was and remains the subject of much controversy in Britain.[18] Despite a decisive rejection of the Conservative party in the spring 1997 elections, the new Labour Prime Minister Blair has evidently adopted a number of elements of the Tory programme with its emphasis on individual responsibility, personal incentives and private enterprise, and competition in the marketplace.

It is not an exaggeration to say that the Tory programme has never been the agenda of mainstream Irish politicians. Perhaps this was given by circumstances at the time. Ireland was overshadowed by a more immediate and pressing set of problems in the 1980s: how to reduce a massive fiscal haemorrhage, get the national debt under control and, most importantly, to credibly reduce inflation (Dornbusch 1989). In a blast of tight monetary and fiscal policy, Ireland managed to reduce its debt/GDP ratio by more than 20 percentage points to under 75% in 1997, an outstanding achievement, while reducing its inflation rate to under 2% at the same time. Ireland looks like a shoe-in for the European Monetary Union in 1999, regardless of what form this union ultimately takes.

This blast of fiscal rectitude in Ireland was pragmatic, driven by the need to get the public debt under control as well as the desire to enter the EMS and participate in any future form of monetary integration. In sharp contrast to the UK, there was no paradigmatic change in the way politicians and voters think about the state (Beam and Symons 1989). There was little or no public discussion of rolling back the role of the state as was the case with Tory Party rhetoric in Britain. While the stabilisation programme succeeded - in defiance of the naysayers (see Dornbusch 1989) - it would be inaccurate to assert that Ireland had its own Tory Revolution. Unlike the UK, the political rhetoric accompanying the changes did not call for a dumping of the social welfare system.

---

[18] For an early critical assessment of the Thatcher years see Bean and Symons, 1989. For a somewhat partisan view, see Matthews and Minford, 1987.

Despite philosophical differences concerning the role of the state, it is illuminating to examine the net effects of Thatcher's rule compared with the cumulative outcome of the Fitzgerald, Haughey, Reynolds and Bruton governments. Table 7 presents a comparison of various indicators of the government's presence in the economy for averages in both countries over the periods 1980-4 and 1990-4. Several surprising facts are revealed.

Table 7   The Rollback of the State in Ireland and United Kingdom, in % of GDP

	Ireland		United Kingdom	
	1980-1984	**1990-1994**	**1980-1984**	**1990-1994**
Government Spending	46.0	41.1	43.3	41.0
Government Purchases	18.6	15.8	22.0	21.5
Transfers	16.2	17.1	14.2	15.0
of which:				
- Social Security Benefits	6.1	5.0	6.8	6.2
- Social Assistance Grants	7.9	10.0	4.6	6.3
Subsidies	3.5	1.1	2.3	1.1
Taxes:				
- Indirect Taxes	16.0	14.8	16.0	14.2
- Direct Taxes	12.8	15.1	14.8	13.2

Source: OECD, *National Accounts*, Vol. II, various issues

First, despite the rhetoric of the UK government about reducing the size and scope of government, Irish fiscal policy has in fact been more stringent than Britain's. Over the period I examine, the fraction of total government outlays fell in the UK by only 2.3% of GDP; in Ireland it declined by almost 5%. The faster decline in Ireland may, in part, reflect the much faster growth in Irish GDP. Second, the Irish cuts fell primarily on government purchases of goods and services, which declined by almost three percentage points of GDP; in sharp contrast, government's claim on output in the UK hardly changed over the period. As the table shows, the modest reduction in government in the UK was via a reduction in subsidies and government purchases. Overall, transfers to households actually *increased* over the period in both countries, especially in

Ireland. More striking is the form in which the increase occurred. While social security benefits in Ireland - which are earnings-related - fell from 6.1% to 5%, social assistance, or unconditional welfare assistance, rose from 7.9% to 10%. Transfers in Ireland now represent one-tenth of all productive value-added generated. At the same time, subsidies to enterprises in both countries were cut dramatically, in Ireland by more than 2% of GDP. (The UK policies, however, involved a dramatic transfer from government to the private ownership of state-owned firms as is documented in the contribution by Vickers to this volume.)

4.2 *An Unemployment/Fiscal Trap in Ireland?*

The central difference between the UK and Ireland - which relates to the ideology issue - is how both countries implemented their respective fiscal austerity programmes. In my opinion, this difference plays a central role in Ireland's persistent unemployment problem. The UK reduced the share of taxes in the economy by more than 3% of GDP, while Ireland *increased* its overall total tax burden by one percentage point, in particular the direct tax burden rose by 2.3%. This has tended to fall on labour and consumption rather than capital (Dornbusch 1989). While this may have the advantage of attracting foreign capital, it renders labour less attractive for firms. At the same time, the collective bargaining system of Ireland allows labour to protect its net income by shifting increases in income taxes forward onto wages - increasing after tax costs, and leading to more unemployment, a greater claim on the social budget and once again higher taxes. Herein lies a disadvantage of a strong union sector, although the recent move to corporatism vitiates this effect, to the extent that unions anticipate and internalise interactions of taxation, labour costs, and unemployment (Burda 1997).

Figure 5 shows how direct and indirect taxation have evolved in the aggregate (as a percentage of GDP) since the early 1970s. It is evident that the UK has not only prevented 'creeping contributions' and increasing labour taxation, but has reduced direct taxes significantly. In Ireland, labour taxes - income taxes and social security contributions - have risen secularly.

Figure 5 Direct and Indirect Taxes as % of GDP

Ireland   **United Kingdom**

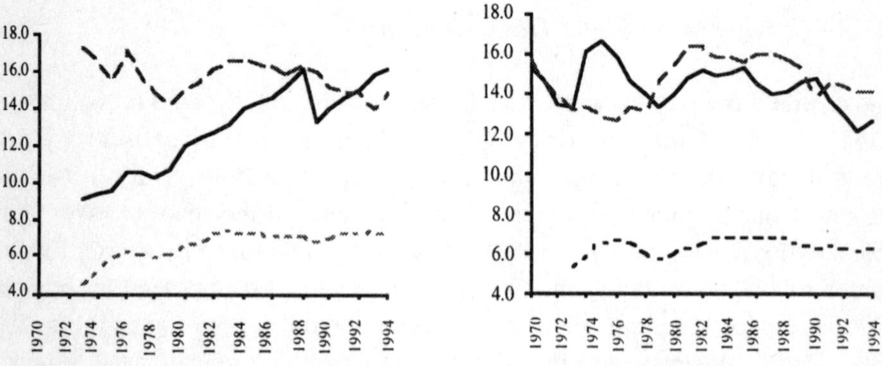

_____ Direct Taxes   _ _ _ Indirect Taxes   - - - - Social Security Contribution

Source: OECD, *National Accounts*, Vol. II, various issues.

The second half of the Irish problem is the 'unemployment trap'. Originally associated with Minford (1985) and often discounted as Tory propaganda, the idea has received renewed attention in policy circles as an important factor determining labour supply, especially for unskilled, low-wage earners.[19] The idea is simply that the work decision involves the foregoing of so many benefits that the effective tax rate on labour income can exceed 100%, conditions under which no rational actor would take up work. Originally described with respect to unemployment benefits, the problem is even more severe for social assistance, and applies especially to families in which both adults are unemployed.

---

[19] One original contribution in this area was Burtless and Hapsman, 1978. See Gregg and Wadsworth, 1995 for an application to low-pay workers in the UK.

The OECD has recently recognised this problem in its 1996 *Employment Outlook,* in which estimates of marginal effective tax rates for benefit recipients are reported (OECD 1996: 44). Of the seven countries studied, Ireland had the highest marginal effective tax rate in the table at 105%; moreover, this applied to workers earning as much as 62-76% of average earnings. This compares rather poorly with Britain, where the effective marginal tax rate ranged from 80.5% (for workers earning 65-77% of average wages) to 97% (for workers earning 46-65% of average earnings).[20] In the United States the rate applying to comparable earnings ranges was estimated at only 72%. In Ireland, the high effective marginal tax rates are driven by social security taxes (5%), income taxes (40%) and family income supplement (60%).[21]

The unemployment trap not only neutralises the incentive to take up work paying gross rates which do not compensate for the forfeiture of benefit, but also has the side effect of increasing wage compression at the lowest end of the pay scale, since many low wage jobs are never created. In addition, it should be stressed that the problem is generally unaffected and may even be aggravated by overall income tax cuts, since they do not generally affect the lowest income brackets. While it is beyond the purview of this essay to explore the microeconomics of the fiscal unemployment trap, there is sufficient evidence from Britain and other countries to justify increased concern on the part of Irish policymakers as well as the diversion of more academic resources to studying the practical importance of this issue.[22]

---

[20] Important factors determining the difference between the two in the UK are the housing benefit and council tax benefits (applicable to the poorer family).

[21] The OECD calculation does not account for a number of benefits available to Irish families under social assistance, such as butter vouchers, housing allowances, fuel allowances, smokeless fuel allowances, free electricity allowances, free natural gas allowances, free bottled gas refill allowances, free television licence allowances, free telephone rental allowances, back-to-school clothing and footwear allowances. Certainly these items could help explain the increase in social welfare transfers in the past decade!

[22] This was also the recommendation of the OECD in their 1997 *Economic Survey.* To be fair, the Irish government has recently picked up on this issue, lowering social security contributions for low wage workers, improving the Family Income Supplement for working parents, and introducing the Back to Work Allowance Scheme; nevertheless the Survey stresses the need to reform the marginal relief system, which in itself imposes a 47% marginal effective tax rate and applies to an eighth of all taxpayers (OECD 1997).

5   Conclusion

Ireland poses an interesting economic experiment - or at least a case study - for several reasons. It is a small open economy with an exceptionally large agricultural sector - which certainly reflects to some extent its comparative advantage - but which was subject to the 'Spanish problem': Ireland entered the EU in 1973 at a time when the agricultural sector was still too large for sustainability and the manufacturing sector was on weak legs. Both sectors were decimated in the integration process. Now that both new high wage manufacturing and services are growing rapidly, a fiscal trap seems to be emerging involving the taxation of labour, which is 'nothing short of oppressive' (Dornbusch, 1989:198). This assessment is consistent with a rising pattern of direct taxes on labour over time, and has been aggravated by Ireland's low rate of capital taxation and the exceptionally high priority given to attracting foreign investment.

A comparison of the UK and Ireland over the past twenty-five years suggests that high unemployment in Ireland cannot be attributed to contractionary demand policies of the previous decade. Were this the case, then Ireland would have surely mastered the situation with its recent impressive growth, especially relative to Britain. Instead, the singularly striking fact is an abysmally low employment rate in comparison with the UK, even when gender patterns of labour force participation are taken into account. That the nonemployment rate in Ireland has risen from under 35% in the early 1960s to almost 50% in the late 1980s points to a severe labour market problem with long-run ramifications for fiscal policy and economic efficiency. While labour force participation in Britain has risen since 1980, it has stagnated in Ireland. Females especially have been disadvantaged by this development.

As in other continental economies such as France, Italy, Germany and Spain, the equilibrium or 'natural' rate of unemployment has risen in Ireland. This increase occurred despite a decline of equilibrium unemployment in the UK in the past decade, and despite the extensive degree of economic integration between the two countries. This development portends a 'parting of the ways' that is reflected, among other things, in Ireland's wholehearted endorsement of European Monetary Union despite her trade-love embrace with Britain. Yet the usual structural suspects that could explain the rise in equilibrium or structural unemployment do not fare too well in explaining the divergence. The insider-outsider explanation runs counter to the current view of Irish unions as corporatist institutions. Severance regulations are almost identical to Britain's. While generous, unemployment benefits have been whittled away over time, probably to avoid unwanted competition with the UK along this dimension, with the consequence that the number of individuals receiving social assistance has increased dramatically.

The most promising of all explanations seems to be the 'fiscal-unemployment trap', as it represents the most salient contemporary difference between Ireland and the UK. Neither a purely demand or supply story, the fiscal-unemployment trap has components in both blades of the labour market scissors. First, high rates of labour taxation - a combination of income taxes, social security contributions, and other charges - are shifted forward by unions into labour costs and stunt employment growth, especially in the low-pay sectors and occupations. At the same time, the tax and benefit system in Ireland leaves the unemployed with little improvement from employment - especially low-pay work. Effective marginal tax rates in excess of 100% not only make it irrational to take up work, but also buttress the labour's demands in collective bargaining and support the further forward shifting of labour tax increases. The high level of welfare dependence may have helped the Irish to avoid UK levels of poverty and inequality, but have also necessitated high rates of labour taxation with consequences for job creation. Giving my surprising finding that sectoral wage dispersion in the UK has returned to 1980s levels in the past decade, Irish social policy has served only to 'anaesthetise' low-skilled, less productive workers as the price of maintaining a relatively egalitarian pay structure for those with jobs.[23]

Does Ireland need the type of labour market reforms which were introduced in the UK in the 1980s? This question might appear inappropriate when one regards the painful adjustment borne by the UK over the past two decades. It is, however, worth reflecting on the minimal necessary reforms for eliminating structural rigidities in Ireland. The recent rapid growth of the Irish economy without significant impact on unemployment rates indicates a structural problem, which, while without immediate social consequences, portends the emergence of a two-class society - those with jobs and those without - as has been the case in many other continental European countries. This is a continental development that Ireland could do well to avoid.[24]

---

[23] See Atkinson's contribution in this volume for evidence on the growth in inequality in Ireland in comparison to other European countries.

[24] Dr. Thomas Mitchell, provost of Trinity College, recently raised exactly these issues in a pair of articles appearing in *The Irish Times* (July 23-24, 1997).

References

Ashenfelter, O. and D. Card, 1986, "Why Have Unemployment Rates in Canada and the United States Diverged?", *Economica* (supplement), 53, pp. 171-95.

Barry, F. and J. Bradley, 1991, "On the Causes of Ireland's Unemployment", *The Economic and Social Review*, 22, pp. 253-286.

Bean C. and J. Symons, 1989, "Ten Years of Mrs. T.", *NBER Macroeconomics Annual, 1989*, pp. 13-61.

Blanchard, O.J. and L. Summers, 1986, "Hysteresis and the European Unemployment Problem", *NBER Macroeconomics Annual* 1, pp. 1-78.

Burda, M., 1997, "Corporatism, Labor Unions, and the Safety Net", *European Economic Review* , 411, pp. 635-646.

Burtless, G. and J. Hausman, 1978, "The Effect of Taxation on Labour Supply. Evaluating the Gary Negative Income Tax Experiment", *Journal of Political Economy*, 86, pp. 1103-1130.

Calmfors, L. and J. Driffill, 1988, "Bargaining Structure, Corporatism and Macroeconomic Performance", *Economic Policy,* 6, pp. 13-62.

Dornbusch, R., 1989, "Credibility, Debt and Unemployment: Ireland's Failed Stabilization", *Economic Polic*, 8, pp. 173-201.

European Commission, 1997, *Employment Observatory: Tableau de Bord,* Luxembourg Office for Official Publications of the European Communities.

Galbraith, J., 1997, "Time to Ditch the NAIRU", *Journal of Economic Perspectives,* 11, pp. 93-108.

"Green is Good", *The Economist,* May 17, 1997, pp. 23-26.

Gregg, P. and J. Wadsworth, 1995, "Mind the Gap? The Changing Nature of Entry Jobs in Britain", mimeo, Centre for Economic Performance, London.

Honohan, P., 1992, "The Link between Irish and UK Unemployment", *Quarterly Economic Commentary*, ESRI, Spring, pp. 33-44.

Minford, P., 1985, *Unemployment: Cause and Cure*, second edition, Basil Blackwell, Oxford.

Newell, A. and J. Symons, 1990, "The Cause of Ireland's Unemployment", *The Economic and Social Review,* 21:, pp. 409-429.

Nickell, S., 1996, "Sectoral Structural Change and the State of the Labour Market in Great Britain", Centre for Economic Performance Discussion Paper Series No. 2, May.

OECD, 1995, *Trends in International Migration* report of SOPEMI for 1994, OECD, Paris.

OECD, 1996, *The Employment Outlook*, OECD, Paris.

OECD, 1997, *Economic Survey of Ireland*, OECD, Paris.

Staiger, D., J. Stock and M. Watson, 1997, "The NAIRU, Unemployment and Monetary Policy", *Journal of Economic Perspectives* , 11, pp. 33-50.

St. Paul, G., 1996, "Understanding Labour Market Institutions: A Political Economy Perspective", CEPR DP 1438.

Topel, R., 1986, "Local Labor Markets", *Journal of Political Economy* , 94(3), pp. 111-143.

Walsh, B., 1992, "Appropriate Policy Changes", in A.W.Gray editor, *Responses to Irish Unemployment*, the views of four economists, Indecon, Dublin.

Walsh B., 1996, "Stabilisation and Adjustment in a Small Open Economy: Ireland 1979-95", *Oxford Review of Economic Policy* , 12, pp. 74-86.

The Sources of Irish Growth

Angel de la Fuente and Xavier Vives*
Instituto de Análisis Económico,
CSIC, Barcelona

F43   052 047

1   Introduction

Ireland's economic performance over the last few decades has been rather uneven. During the period 1960-85, Ireland's income per capita remained rather stable relative to the OECD average as the country was surpassed by Japan and Spain and lost considerable ground relative to Greece and Portugal. During the decade 1986-96, by contrast, Ireland exhibited the highest growth rate of the OECD, pulled away from the Mediterranean countries and significantly reduced the income differential with respect to the OECD average. This extraordinary performance has earned Ireland the title of *Europe's tiger economy*.[1]

What factors can explain this dramatic reversal? This paper attempts to provide a tentative "supply-side" answer to this question on the basis of an empirical analysis of the proximate determinants of growth in a sample of industrial economies. We use a growth accounting approach and check how much of the "Irish miracle" can be explained in terms of conventional variables, like investment in different types of capital or *convergence* effects. The residual of the exercise then gives us an indication of the extent to which we have to resort to "special" explanations based on particular Irish features not captured in standard growth models.

*We would like to thank Ramon Caminal, Jordi Gali, Peter Neary and John Sutton for useful conversations and help in preparing this manuscript

---

[1] *The Economist*, May 17th, 1997.

The paper is organised as follows. To set the stage, section 2 reviews the evolution of Ireland's relative income per capita during the last few decades and examines the comparative behaviour of the main immediate determinants of this variable. Next, we introduce and estimate a simple empirical growth model which, building on the recent convergence literature, explicitly relates the evolution of income per capita to investment rates and other variables. This model is then used in a growth accounting exercise which provides quantitative estimates of the immediate sources of Ireland's growth differential vis-à-vis two natural references: the OECD average and two countries which start out from rather similar income levels, Spain and Portugal. Section 3 presents the main results of the exercise, leaving the details of the model and the empirical results for the Appendix. Finally, section 4 discusses the results, provides a tentative interpretation of the factors underlying Ireland's spectacular performance in recent years and concludes with some reflections on the types of policies which may be helpful in maintaining a rapid rate of economic growth.

2 Evolution of Income per Capita and Other Key Variables

The convergence plot shown in Figure 1 provides a convenient point of departure for our analysis of Ireland's growth experience during the last decades. This plot summarises the relationship between the initial position of each country in our sample of 21 industrial economies in terms of relative income per capita (i.e. log GDP per capita in deviations from the contemporaneous sample average of the same variable) and its differential growth rate during the period 1960-95.[2] As expected in this sample, the slope of the fitted regression line is negative, indicating that poorer countries have tended to grow faster than richer ones on average. The situation of each country in relation with the fitted regression line (which describes what may be considered the 'typical' growth pattern in the

---

[2]Ireland's GDP is significantly higher than its GNP because the first measure of national income includes the profits of multinational firms. Since these profits eventually revert to the companies' home countries, GNP is probably a better measure of welfare than GDP. In addition, measured GDP may tend to overstate Ireland's productivity because this indicator may be biased upward, particularly in recent years, by multinational accounting practices which can be expected to artificially shift profits into their Irish subsidiaries in order to benefit from low tax rates. Keating, 1995 (reported in Walsh, 1996), however, shows that adjusting GDP for this effect does not significantly reduce the growth rate of the Irish economy.

sample) can be used as an indicator of a country's growth performance after eliminating a 'convergence effect' which presumably reflects the relative advantages of initially backward countries (such as a higher rate of return on investment if the technology exhibits decreasing returns to scale in reproducible factors, technological diffusion and the ability to shift a large fraction of the labour force out of agriculture and into more productive activities).

During the period 1960-95 Ireland has grown at an annual rate which exceeds the sample average by around 0.80%. Although this positive differential is quite significant in absolute terms, it represents only about average performance given the country's initial situation as the richest of the group of poor OECD economies. Controlling for the convergence effect, Ireland has done somewhat better than the Mediterranean countries in the sample (Portugal, Spain and Greece), but much worse than Japan.

Figure 1 Convergence in Income per Capita in the OECD, 1960-95

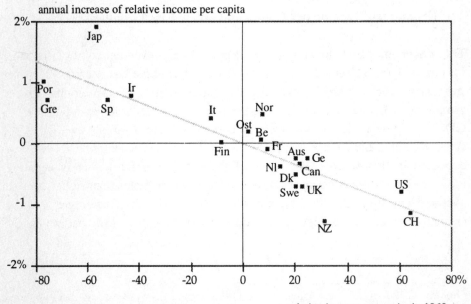

Note: The fitted regression line is given by gyrel.60-95 = 0.00 - 0.01698*lyrel60 t = 7.91, R^2 = 0.7673 where gyrel is the average annual change in relative income and lyrel the initial value of relative income.

Key: Por = Portugal, Gre = Greece, Jap = Japan, Sp = Spain, Ir = Ireland, It = Italy, Fin = Finland, Ost = Austria, Be = Belgium, Nor = Norway, Fr = France, Nl = Netherlands, Dk = Denmark, Swe = Sweden, Aus = Australia, Ge = West Germany, Can = Canada, UK = United Kingdom, NZ = New Zealand, US = United States, CH = Switzerland.

A positive growth differential has enabled Ireland to roughly preserve its initial advantage over the Mediterranean countries and to significantly reduce the income gap with respect to the OECD average. Figure 2, however, shows that progress on this front has been rather uneven. During the 1960s Ireland lost some ground relative to the OECD average and was surpassed by some of its closest 'competitors' within the group of poorer economies. The period 1970-85 was a bit better, with Ireland gaining a few points relative to the sample average and overcoming the Mediterranean countries. Finally, the last decade in our sample was a period of extremely rapid growth in Ireland, which clearly pulls ahead of the pack of the poorer EU economies and approaches the OECD average.[3]

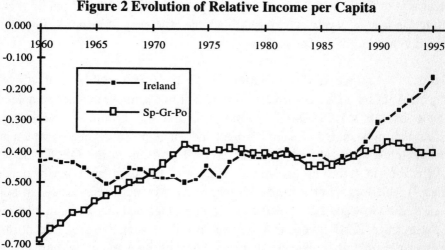

Figure 2 Evolution of Relative Income per Capita

Note: Ireland's relative income per capita is log GDP per capita in deviations from the contemporaneous average value of the same variable in the same sample of 21 OECD economies as in Figure 1. The figure also shows the unweighted average of the relative incomes of Spain, Greece and Portugal.

---

[3]Our GDP figures, as with most of the data used in this paper, are taken from Doménech and Boscá, 1996, who essentially replicate the Summers and Heston data base using a set of OECD-specific purchasing power parities and OECD National Accounts data. As various authors have noted, Ireland's growth profile may be somewhat sensitive to the data set used. O Gráda and O'Rourke, 1994, for example, find significant differences between the series constructed by Maddison and by Summers & Heston during the period 1973-88. The first source, which seems to be based on OECD data (the authors do not provide many details), is rather more optimistic than the second one. Our data appear to be closer to Summers and Heston's, even though they are based on OECD data.

In this paper we will try to 'explain' the growth pattern we have just highlighted in terms of the behaviour of three sets of variables. First of all we will focus on factor accumulation, as described by the rates of investment in physical, human and technological capital, and on the possible impact of two convergence mechanisms identified by the growth literature: the operation of decreasing returns to scale and technological diffusion.[4] In addition to these 'growth theory' variables, we will examine the evolution of two variables which summarise labour market performance (the unemployment and labour force participation rates) and have a direct impact on income per capita for given levels of output per worker. Finally, we will also include among our explanatory variables an indicator of the size of the government sector (total government expenditures as a percentage of GDP) which may serve as a proxy for the effects of public sector activity on income levels, working through the efficiency of resource allocation and individual incentives for work and effort.

Figures 3-8 summarise the evolution of the relevant variables and allow a comparison of Ireland's performance with that of two natural reference samples: a sample of (up to) 21 OECD economies, and the group of low-income Mediterranean countries (Spain, Portugal and where possible Greece) which are Ireland's closest neighbours in terms of their position in the OECD income distribution. In terms of investment rates and labour market performance, Ireland's situation is fairly similar to that of the Mediterranean group. In both cases we find low and falling participation rates, high and rising unemployment, below-average R&D investment and sharply increasing rates of educational investment. Ireland, however, displays rates of investment in human and technological capital which are consistently above those observed in most other low-income countries, and a generally higher unemployment rate.

---

[4]Much of the recent empirical growth literature has focused on the convergence implications of decreasing returns to scale in reproducible factors (see for example Barro and Sala, 1992, and Mankiw, Romer and Weil, 1992). Dowrick and Nguyen, 1989, and de la Fuenté, 1995, examine the implications of cross-country technological diffusion.

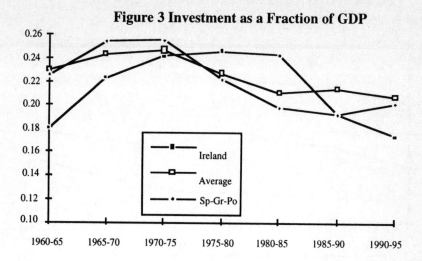

Figure 3 Investment as a Fraction of GDP

Note: Average = unweighted average of the investment rates of the 21 OECD countries included in Figure 1. Sp-Gr-Po = unweighted average of the values for Spain, Greece and Portugal.

Figure 4 Secondary and University Enrolment as a Percentage of the Labour Force

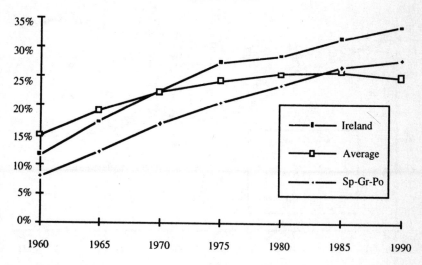

Source: UNESCO, *Yearbook.*

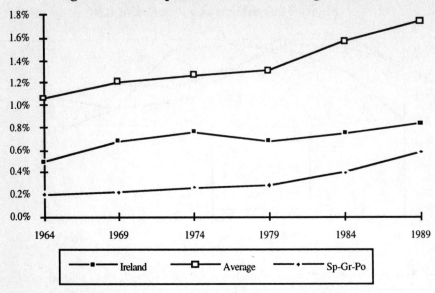

Figure 5 R&D Expenditures as a Percentage of GDP

Source: UNESCO *Yearbook,* and *Basic Science and Technology Statistics.*

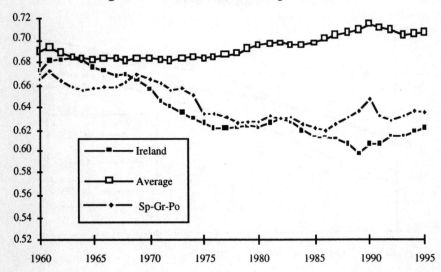

Figure 6 Labour Force Participation Rate

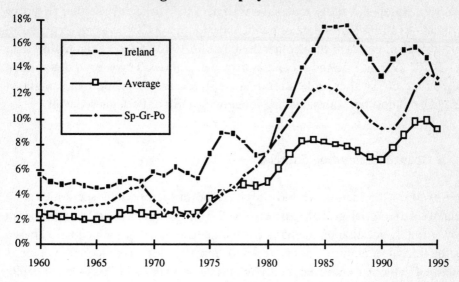

Figure 7 Unemployment Rate

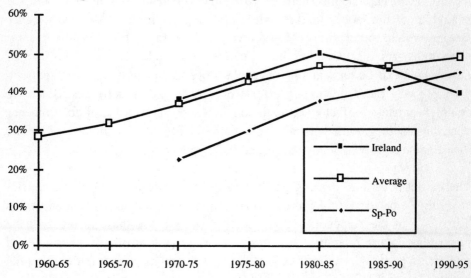

Figure 8 Government Spending as a Percentage of GDP

Note: Average over each five-year period. The OECD average is taken over all countries for which data are available in each period. Switzerland and New Zealand are excluded for lack of data, and data for Greece start in 1980-85.
Source: OECD Statistical Compendium and European Commission.

In terms of public finances, however, the pattern is very different. Ireland seems to have developed a fairly extensive welfare state earlier than either Spain or Portugal. As a result, the share of public expenditure in GDP was much higher in Ireland than in either of these other countries in 1970-75 (and even higher than the OECD average). In the second half of the 'eighties, however, a determined programme of fiscal consolidation reduced the share of public expenditure in Ireland by almost ten points, leaving it below Spanish or Portuguese levels.

3   A Growth Accounting Exercise

How well do the factors we have highlighted in the previous section explain Ireland's differential growth performance? This section will try to provide an answer to this question on the basis of a simple empirical growth equation based on the recent literature on growth and convergence. The model, which is described in the Appendix, explicitly relates the growth rate of income per capita in each country with its rates of accumulation of physical, human and technological capital, the share of government expenditures in GDP and the behaviour of the labour market, while allowing for some of the *convergence factors* which, other things equal, would tend to favour initially poorer economies. As discussed in the Appendix, the inclusion of a measure of government expenditures among the explanatory variables attempts to capture in a simple way the distortionary effects of various public activities. Since we control separately for factor accumulation, however, our measure of government's contribution to growth will not include the direct positive impact of public investment on growth, or any adverse crowding out effects.

The model is estimated using panel data for a sample of 19 OECD countries covering the period 1965-95 at five-year intervals with the results summarised in Table A.1 of the Appendix. In this section we will use these results and the underlying data to quantify the contribution to growth of different variables of interest. In particular, we will decompose each country's growth rate differential with respect to the OECD average into seven factors which reflect, respectively:

(a)   a convergence effect (CONV) which results from the operation of decreasing returns to scale and technological diffusion and tends to favour initially backward countries;

120

(b)   the impact of labour market performance on income per capita (LAB, which summarises the contributions to growth of income per capita of changes in the unemployment and labour force participation rates);

(c)-(e) the contribution of factor accumulation (investment in physical (K), human (H) and technological (R&D) capital), normalised by population growth in the manner suggested by the model;

(f)   the impact of government size (measured by the share of total expenditures in GDP) on productivity (GOV); and

(g)   an error term which is the difference between the observed growth rate differential and the model's prediction for each country and period.

Table 1 summarises the results of the exercise for the case of Ireland and for a fictional country constructed as an unweighted average of Spain and Portugal (Greece is excluded because full data for this country are available only after 1980). The first two columns of the table show the observed (OBS) growth rate in income per capita in differences with the contemporaneous sample average (excluding Greece), and the model's prediction for the same variable (PRED). The remaining columns report the seven components of the differential growth rate described above. The first group of rows displays averages for the period 1970-95. The second and third groups break down this period into the subperiods 1970-85 and 1985-95. In all three cases, the growth rates of Ireland and our fictional average Latin country are expressed in differences with the sample average, and the last row in each group shows the difference between these two figures *(difference)*, which measures Ireland's performance relative to the average of Spain and Portugal. The last group of rows (Δ) displays the change in Ireland's performance relative to the OECD average *(Ireland)* and to the Latin countries *(difference)* between the first and second subperiods. Finally, Figure 9 shows a more detailed, period-by-period breakdown of the components of Ireland's growth differential with the OECD average. As can be seen in the graph, the convergence effect is initially positive and very large but declines rapidly throughout the period. This negative change is partially offset by the improved contribution of the government sector and the rise in human capital investment. These effects, however, are not sufficient to explain Ireland's extraordinary performance during the last part of the period, leaving us with a large positive residual term for the subperiod 1990-95.

Table 1 Sources of Differential Growth, 1970-95

		OBS	PRED	LAB	CONV	K	H	R&D	GOV	ERROR
Ireland	1970-95	1.17%	1.25%	-0.20%	1.34%	-0.07%	0.12%	-0.18%	0.25%	-0.08%
Po&Sp	1970-95	0.33%	0.18%	-0.36%	1.35%	-0.06%	-0.27%	-0.47%	-0.03%	0.16%
Difference	1970-95	0.84%	1.08%	0.16%	0.00%	-0.01%	0.39%	0.29%	0.28%	-0.24%
Ireland	1970-85	0.39%	0.93%	-0.54%	1.83%	-0.05%	-0.04%	-0.20%	-0.07%	-0.54%
Po&Sp	1970-85	-0.10%	-0.12%	-0.70%	1.74%	-0.18%	-0.48%	-0.51%	-0.01%	0.02%
Difference	1970-85	0.49%	1.05%	0.16%	0.09%	0.13%	0.44%	0.31%	-0.06%	-0.56%
Ireland	1985-95	2.34%	1.74%	0.31%	0.61%	-0.10%	0.36%	-0.16%	0.72%	0.61%
Po&Sp	1985-95	0.98%	0.62%	0.16%	0.76%	0.12%	0.05%	-0.41%	-0.06%	0.35%
Difference	1985-95	1.37%	1.12%	0.15%	-0.15%	-0.21%	0.31%	0.25%	0.78%	0.25%
Ireland	Δ	1.95%	0.81%	0.85%	-1.22%	-0.05%	0.40%	0.04%	0.78%	1.14%
Difference	Δ	0.88%	0.07%	0.00%	-0.24%	-0.34%	-0.13%	-0.06%	0.84%	0.81%

Moving on to table 1, the figures shown in the first group of rows refer to average performance over the entire period 1970-95. The small residual (-0.08%) shows that when we consider the sample period as a whole the model explains rather well Ireland's performance relative to the OECD average and the Latin countries. The positive growth differential with the OECD (1.17%) seems to be due mostly to the positive contribution of the convergence effects (1.34%). The factor accumulation components of the growth rate are negative (with the exception of human capital) and rather small, while labour market performance (-0.20%) and government's contribution (0.25%) roughly offset each other. The pattern is qualitatively similar in the case of Spain and Portugal, but with some differences which help account for the 0.84% positive differential in Ireland's favour. In particular, relatively high rates of investment in education and R&D and a lower rate of growth in the share of government expenditures contributed around a third of a point each to this differential.

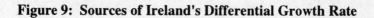

Figure 9: Sources of Ireland's Differential Growth Rate

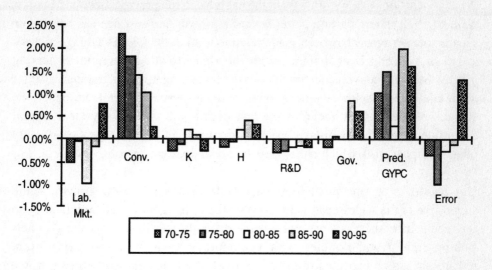

If we take the sample period as a whole, then, the sources of Ireland's relative growth performance seem fairly straightforward: convergence towards the OECD average was fuelled mostly by the usual convergence effects, and the positive differential with respect to the Latin countries reflected mostly a higher rate of factor accumulation and a greater degree of fiscal discipline. When we disaggregate into subperiods, however, the story becomes rather less clear. As shown in the last two rows of the table, Ireland's growth differential with respect to the OECD average increases by 1.95% between the first and second subperiods. The model explains around half of this increase in terms of improved labour market performance (0.85%), a reduction in the convergence effect (-1.22%), increased investment in human capital (0.40%) and greater fiscal discipline (0.78%), but this still leaves us with a residual of over a percentage point per year. The problem is similar when we compare Ireland's growth to that of Spain and Portugal: the positive contribution of the government term (0.84%) just about offsets the negative contributions of the convergence effects (-0.24%) and factor accumulation (-0.43%), leaving us with an unexplained residual of 0.81% per year.

4 An Interpretation and Future Perspectives

What conclusions can we draw from the exercise in the previous section? First, if we take 1970 as our starting point, Ireland's growth performance has been quite satisfactory. Progress has been made relative to both the OECD average and the group of poorer EU economies, with the first growth differential reflecting mainly the usual convergence forces and the second relatively high rates of factor accumulation and below-average growth of the government sector. Secondly, the sources of the 'Irish miracle' of the last decade are not entirely clear. Fiscal discipline seems to have played an important role in it, but there are probably other factors at work which our aggregate model does not capture.

Our results about the positive impact of fiscal discipline on growth, while supportive of the widespread view that this factor has contributed significantly to the recent Irish success story, raise some difficult questions about the channels linking tight fiscal policies with economic growth. Tax and expenditure reductions can be expected to increase growth by reducing disincentives which tend to depress investment and labour supply. King and Rebelo, 1990, show that the impact on output of these effects can be quite important, especially in the case of a small open economy. Since we are controlling for both employment and factor accumulation, however, what our estimates are presumably picking up are not these effects, or the "crowding out" of private investment, but a negative externality effect of government size on the efficiency of resource allocation and on work effort. From this perspective, the estimated effects are surprisingly large, particularly when we consider that fiscal tightening in Ireland has not been accompanied by the comprehensive microeconomic reforms which may conceivably have triggered such large efficiency gains. On the other hand, there is some support in the literature for the view that taxation and other policies which distort resource allocation may have large adverse effects on productivity (see for example Jorgenson and Yun, 1986 and 1990). Other models also suggest additional links between fiscal policy and growth which may help account for our results. Olson and other authors, for instance, have argued that large governments may be linked with slow growth through rent-seeking behaviour (see Benabou, 1996). In a different line, Bertola and Drazen, 1993, have shown that fiscal contractions can have an expansionary effect, working through private consumption and possibly investment, if they trigger expectations of a permanent reduction in government expenditure and tax levels. Indeed, Bertola and Drazen, 1993, as Giavazzi and Pagano, 1990, focus on the Irish experience as a paradigmatic case of such an expansionary fiscal consolidation.

While our analysis does not allow us to identify the channels through which such a policy may affect growth, our results do suggest that the contractionary effects of a reduction in government expenditures predicted by standard Keynesian-type models seem to be outweighted on the average by forces working in the opposite direction. Further research is needed to clarify just what these forces are.

Coming back to the Irish case, our results are consistent with the view that fiscal adjustment was directly responsible for a sizeable increase in the growth rate. But this still leaves much of the improvement in Ireland's economic performance unexplained. The large remaining residual in our analysis suggests that factors not considered by our model have played an important role and points us towards specifically Irish characteristics. As far as these go, the dominant view in the literature seems to be that rapid growth has been driven mostly by a very dynamic export sector dominated by multinational firms which have invested heavily in Ireland in recent years and served as a conduit for the adoption of advanced technologies.[5] This boom in foreign direct investment would reflect Ireland's attractiveness as a natural base for exports to the European Union. This attractiveness would be due in part to the provision of generous tax incentives which may have served to compensate for other disadvantages such as high prices for business services and other inputs to manufacturing.[6] Other important factors would be the availability of a highly skilled and English-speaking labour force, relatively low labour costs (preserved in recent years by an incomes policy aimed at wage moderation), heavy investment in infrastructure and a pragmatic exchange rate policy. An additional consideration is the inflow of large subsidies from the European Union (peaking in 1979 at 6% of GDP and then gradually falling to slightly below 4%), which has helped to finance infrastructure and educational investment without undue budget strain.

---

[5] See, for example, O Grada and O'Rourke, 1994, Walsh. 1996, Leddin and Walsh, 1997, and *The Economist*, May 17th, 1997.

[6] Subsidies to the manufacturing sector are quite important. For example, subsidies represented 6.4% of GDP in 1986-88 and 4.9% in 1988-90, while the EU average was 4% and 3.5%, respectively. See OECD, 1993.

This story has a ring of plausibility to it and indeed it is difficult to think of a convincing alternative explanation. It may be asked, however, why success came when it did. After all, many of the factors we have just cited have been in operation for quite a few years before the current growth spurt.[7] We would venture the guess that the success in attracting foreign direct investment in recent years was triggered by two factors. The first one is the renewed interest of American and other multinational firms in gaining a foothold in Europe which came with the impulse to the EEC represented by the accession of new members in 1986 and the formulation of clear plans for the completion of the Single Market in 1992. The second factor is Ireland's clear bet for macroeconomic stability and its commitment to a sustainable fiscal policy. In this sense, fiscal consolidation may have acted as a catalyst, helping to change foreign investors' perception of the country.

There seems to be some concern in Ireland about the sustainability of the current growth rates (in excess of 6%) and about the potential dangers of a growth strategy based on the attraction of foreign direct investment.[8] Two of the main concerns are the probable loss of Ireland's status as an Objective 1 region as it approaches the European Union's average income per capita, and the prospect that existing tax benefits will be severely limited in the future. The loss of Structural Fund grants from the EU would represent a substantial loss of resources for public investment and training, and it is feared that a less attractive fiscal regime may diminish the country's attractiveness for foreign firms.

Since the current regime of high subsidies to the manufacturing sector may in fact have rather perverse effects on the efficiency of resource allocation, the imposed reduction of existing aids may in fact turn out to be a blessing in disguise. In order to realise its potential, however, it will be necessary to implement policies designed to offset the negative impact of the loss of tax breaks through an improvement in other determinants of competitiveness.[9] From this perspective, the real bottleneck may be then the lack of competition in the service sectors.

---

[7]Ireland joined the EEC in 1973 and has always been a net recipient of aid from the Community. Irish industrial policy has followed since the 'sixties an aggressive policy of promoting foreign direct investment in export-oriented sectors. The relief to the exporting sector turned into a low corporate tax (10%) for the manufacturing sector in 1981, which was then extended to some traded financial services. Other tax relief measures included fixed asset grants and accelerated capital allowances. (See Ruane and Goerg, 1997, for a discussion of Irish industrial policy).

[8]See, for example, Leddin and Walsh, 1997.

[9] The Irish Government has recently established a National Competitiveness Council focused on this issue and reporting directly to the Irish Prime Minister.

Indeed, the fact that Ireland is a small open economy does not help to discipline non-tradables. Ireland has a manufacturing sector open to international competition but favoured with large state subsidies, a service (non-traded) sector with a low level of competition (and no corporate tax discount), and a heavily regulated public enterprise sector. There is evidence that the level of competition in the Irish economy is low. For example, the OECD's 1993 Economic Survey of Ireland provides evidence of high relative costs and prices in Ireland (with respect to other countries) in transportation, communication, food and health care, worries about vertical restraints in retailing and finds barriers to entry in a host of industries including telecommunications, energy, banking, insurance and financial services. The Survey also finds that public firms tend to be inefficient. There is consensus that until 1991, when the passage of the Competition Act adapted Irish legislation to the Treaty of Rome, competition policy was ineffective in Ireland. Since then some progress has been made, with a considerable strengthening of competition law through the 1996 Amendment, but there is still a long way to go in this area (see Fingleton, 1996).

All this means that there is no way around increasing competition in the service sectors if Ireland is to maintain a competitive edge. As usual, this is a painful process. Not because consumers do not gain - they are indeed the major beneficiaries of such a move - but because of the vested interests which have consolidated privileged positions over the years, and consequently have the resources to try to keep those privileges. The objection that an active competition policy would decrease total employment is unfounded. On the contrary, it will tend to increase it.[10] A larger degree of competition in the overall economy and, in particular, in the service sector, would put Ireland in a sustainable growth track provided sound macroeconomic (fiscal and monetary) policies are pursued. This is why we think that the enforcement of competition policy is one of the major and most important challenges ahead for Ireland.

---

[10]See Barry and O'Toole, 1997.

Appendix: An Empirical Growth Model

This Appendix sketches the empirical model which underlies the growth accounting exercise reported in section 3 of the text and summarises the most important results of the estimation. For a full discussion, the interested reader is referred to de la Fuente, 1997a.

Following the usual procedure in the recent empirical growth literature,[11] we derive an empirical convergence equation from a log-linear approximation to a simple growth model. We assume that the production side of the economy can be described by a reduced-form aggregate production function of the form

$$(1) \ Y_{it} = \theta^{\gamma} K_{it}^{\alpha k} H_{it}^{\alpha h} R_{it}^{\alpha r} (A_{it} L_{it})^{1-\alpha k-\alpha h-\alpha r},$$

where Y_{it} is aggregate output in country i at time t, L the level of employment and A_{it} an indicator of the level of technical efficiency which grows at an exponential rate g. The variables K, H and R denote, respectively, the stocks of physical, human and technological capital, and θ is an indicator of the relative weight of the government sector in the economy.

This formulation is completely standard except that it allows national output to be a function of the relative size of government. The 'government externality' term (θ^{γ}) is meant to capture in the simplest possible way the fact that public activities may affect productivity in a variety of ways other than through infrastructure investment, which contributes directly to factor accumulation. Since some of the relevant effects are positive and others negative, the sign of the coefficient γ is unclear ex ante, and may conceivably change with the expenditure level.

---

[11] See for example Barro and Sala, 1992, and Mankiw, Romer and Weil, 1992.

Under the assumptions that the workforce is equal to population and the depreciation rate is constant and equal for all types of capital, it is easy to derive a *convergence equation* of the form:

$$(2) \quad GYPC_{it} = g + \beta a_{it} - \beta * LYPC_{it} + \gamma \left(\dot{\theta}_{it} + (\delta+g+n)\theta_{it} \right)$$

$$+ (\delta+g+n)\left(\alpha_k \ln \frac{S_{kit}}{\delta+g+n_{it}} + \alpha_h \ln \frac{S_{hit}}{\delta+g+n_{it}} + \alpha_r \ln \frac{S_{rit}}{\delta+g+n_{it}} \right)$$

where $GYPC_{it}$ is the growth rate of income per capita in country i during the subperiod which starts at t, LYPC the log of income per capita at the beginning of the subperiod, s_{jit} the fraction of GDP invested in capital of type j (=k, h, r), n_{it} the rate of population growth, a_{it} the log of the indicator of technical efficiency (A_{it}), $\theta = \ln \theta$ the log of government's share in GDP, and δ the rate of depreciation. The coefficient β measures the rate of convergence towards a pseudo-steady state which would be attained asymptotically if the rate of population growth, the share of government expenditures in GDP and the different investment rates remained constant over time. The value of the convergence coefficient will depend on the degree of returns to scale in the reproducible factors (i.e. in the different types of capital), with convergence being faster the faster diminishing returns set in.

Before proceeding to its estimation, we extend equation (2) so as to incorporate some important determinants of growth not considered by the theoretical model from which we start. Since we will work with data on income per capita rather than output per worker, we will include in the equation the increase in the unemployment and labour force participation rates, as changes in these variables would affect income per capita with a constant level of output per employed worker. Secondly, we will control in a simple way for a technological catch-up effect. As discussed in de la Fuente, 1995, if technology diffuses across countries at a sufficiently rapid pace, those economies which are technically less advanced at the beginning of the period should grow faster than the rest. This effect, however, will gradually exhaust itself as each country approaches an equilibrium level of relative technical efficiency which is determined by its own R&D effort and the speed of diffusion. To try to capture this effect we include a dummy for initially backward countries (Spain, Ireland, Greece, Portugal and Japan) and the product of this variable and a trend. We would expect the coefficient of the first variable to be positive, and that of the second to be negative.

With these changes, the equation to be estimated is of the form

(3) $GYPC_{it} = \Gamma_0 + \Gamma_1 * t + \Gamma_2 * t^2 + \Gamma_3 * DLAG5 + \Gamma_4 * DLAG5 * t + \Gamma_a * GTAC_{it} +$
$+ \Gamma_u * DU_{it} - \beta * LYPC_{it} + \gamma \; (GGOV_{it} + (\delta + g + n) \ln GOV_{it})$

$$+ (\delta + g + n) \left(\alpha_k \ln \frac{S_{kit}}{\delta + g + n_{it}} + \alpha_h \ln \frac{S_{hit}}{\delta + g + n_{it}} + \alpha_r \ln \frac{S_{rit}}{\delta + g + n_{it}} \right)$$

where (θ =) GOV is total government expenditure as a fraction of GDP, GGOV the growth rate of this variable, DU the average annual increase in the unemployment rate during the subperiod and GTAC the growth rate of the labour force participation rate (labour force over working-age population). The first terms of the equation (a constant, a trend and a trend squared and the terms which include the dummy DLAG5) try to approximate the term $g + \beta a_{it}$ which appears in equation (2) while allowing for some country heterogeneity.

Following the standard practice in the literature, we will impose a value of $\delta + g$ equal to 0.05. We will also assume that the convergence parameter β is constant over time and across countries (even though the theoretical model suggests that it may vary with the rate of population growth) and will therefore interpret the variable n which enters the term $(\delta + g + n)$ ($= (\beta / (1 - \alpha_k - \alpha_h - \alpha_r))$) that multiplies the logs of the investment rates as the average rate of population growth in the sample as a whole. These simplifying assumptions have the advantage that they make the coefficients which multiply initial income and the logs of the investment rates constant, a feature which facilitates the growth accounting exercise undertaken in the text.

Our data on real income per capita, employment, investment and population growth are taken from Doménech and Boscá, 1996, who essentially replicate the Summers-Heston database for the OECD, using a set of OECD-specific PPPs. Our proxy for the level of investment in human capital (s_h) will be the total secondary and university enrolment as a fraction of the labour force (from the UNESCO Yearbook). The series on R&D expenditure is constructed combining information from the UNESCO Yearbooks and the OECD's *Basic Science and Technology Statistics* as discussed in de la Fuente, 1997a. The last two variables are averaged over several subperiods because it is expected that investment in education and R&D will affect output only with relatively long lags. In the case of s_h we use the average value over the current five-year subperiod and the previous one, and for R&D (s_r) the cumulative average share of total R&D

expenditure in GDP over the current and all preceding subperiods. Finally, our data on government expenditures are taken from the OECD's Statistical Compendium and from CEE, 1996. Due to the lack of fiscal data, we have had to exclude Switzerland and New Zealand from the original sample. With this omission, our sample covers 19 countries and ends in 1990-95. In most cases the first observation corresponds to the period 1965-70 or 1970-75. The exception is Greece, whose first observation corresponds to the subperiod 1980-85.

Table A.1 summarises the results. Following de la Fuente, 1997a,b, equation (3) is estimated jointly with an investment equation using a SUR procedure. Although we will not make much use of this second equation in this paper, this method allows us to increase the precision of the estimates by taking into account the correlation between the error terms of the two equations. The results, and in particular the coefficient of the public expenditure variable, are robust to the use of instrumental variables to correct for a potential endogeneity bias.

Table A.1 Empirical results

(dependent variable) =)	parameter	GYPC	(t)	s_k	(t)
constant	Γ_0	0.0835	(4.60)	0.0987	(1.61)
trend: t	Γ_1	-0.00104	(2.15)	0.0059	(5.10)
trend^2: t^2	Γ_2	$2.94*10^{-5}$	(2.41)	-0.00013	(4.85)
technology gap: DLAG5	Γ_3	0.0188	(3.72)		
tech. gap* trend: DLAG5*t	Γ_4	-0.00098	(4.71)		
growth of participation rate: GTAC	Γ_a	0.5267	(4.44)		
change in unemployment: DU	Γ_u	-0.6496	(4.54)		
log initial income per capita: LYPC	$-\beta$	-0.03394	(5.25)	-0.0413	(4.12)
invest. in physical cap.: $\ln s_k/(\delta+g+n)$	α_k	0.3065	(5.07)		
invest. in human capital: $\ln s_h/(\delta+g+n)$	α_h	0.2041	(3.74)		
R&D investment: $\ln s_r/(\delta+g+n)$	α_r	0.0603	(2.22)		
gov't spend.: $(GGOV+(\delta+g+n) \ln GOV)$	γ	-0.1789	(4.51)	-0.3209	(8.41)
	R^2	0.7817		0.9420	(10.69)
	N	103		99	

Notes: t statistics in parentheses next to each coefficient. N is the number of observations.
The investment equation (with dependent variable s_k) includes as regressors, in addition to the variables shown in the table, the rate of population growth (+), the dependency ratio (total population/employment (-)), the fraction of the population aged 15 to 64 (+), and index of the relative price of capital goods, government transfers to households (+), current subsidies to enterprises (+) and the level of public investment (+), with the last three variables measured as shares of GDP. Country dummies for Ireland (-), Norway (+), US (-), UK (-), Austria (+) and Spain (-) are also included. The sign shown in parentheses next to each variable is that of its estimated coefficient.

The coefficients of the different regressors are significant, have the expected sign and present reasonable values. Thus, the coefficient of the stock of technological capital in the production function (0.0603) is similar to the one obtained by Lichtenberg, 1992, and those of physical and human capital (0.306 and 0.204 respectively) and the convergence rate (0.034) are within the usual range in the literature. The coefficients of the terms which include the technological backwardness dummy are significant and have the expected sign. The values of these coefficients suggest that the contribution of technological diffusion to the growth of the poorer countries was quite important at the beginning of the sample period (around 1.8% per year) but has declined rapidly with the passage of time.

As for the remaining regressors, the coefficients of the changes in the rates of unemployment and labour force participation have the expected sign but their size is smaller than expected. Since both coefficients should be close to one (in absolute value) if labour were a homogeneous factor, the estimated values of the parameters suggest that the 'quality' of the marginal entrant into the labour force or the stock of employed workers is significantly lower than that of the average employed worker. Finally, the coefficient of the government size variable is negative, significant and quite large. While the sign of this coefficient is not surprising in view of the previous literature,[12] its size is considerably larger than we expected - particularly because, since we are controlling for factor accumulation and the level of employment, the distortionary effects we are picking up exclude crowding out and adverse labour supply responses. One possibility we have considered is an endogeneity bias. De la Fuente, 1997b, however, investigates this possibility with some care and concludes that the results do not seem to be driven by reverse causation. Hence, an increase in the size of the public sector seems to have a negative and quite sizeable effect on the level of productivity, even after controlling for employment and factor stocks. The analysis, however, sheds no light on the mechanisms behind this effect.

---

[12] See for example Landau, 1983, 1985 and 1986, and Barro 1991a,b. Levine and Renelt, 1992, and Andrés et al, 1996, however, find that the partial correlation between growth and most fiscal indicators is not robust, in the sense that these variables often lose their significance when additional macroeconomic indicators are included in the growth equation.

References

Alesina, A. and R. Perotti, 1995, "Fiscal Expansions and Adjustments in OECD Countries", *Economic Policy*, 21, pp. 207-248.

Andrés, J., R. Doménech and C. Molinas, 1996, "Macroeconomic Performance and Convergence in OECD countries", Working paper no. 96-02, Universidad de Valencia.

Barro, R. and X. Sala, 1992, "Convergence", *Journal of Political Economy*, 100, 2, pp. 223-251

Barro, R., 1991a, "Economic Growth in a Cross Section of Countries", *Quarterly Journal of Economics*, CVI (2), May, pp. 407-443.

Barro, R., 1991b, "A Cross-Country Study of Growth, Saving and Government", in D. Bernheim and J. Shoven, editors, *National Saving and Economic Performance*, NBER and University of Chicago Press, Chicago, IL, pp. 271-301.

Barry, F. and F. O' Toole, "Irish Competition Policy and the Macroeconomy", forthcoming in Stephen Martin, editor, *Competition Policy in the EU*.

Benabou, R., 1996, "Inequality and Growth", CEPR Discussion Paper no. 1450.

Bertola, G. and A. Drazen, 1993, "Trigger Points and Budget Cuts: Explaining the Effects of Fiscal Austerity", *American Economic Review* , 83 (1), pp. 11-26.

de la Fuente, A., 1995, "Catch-up, Growth and Convergence in the OECD", CEPR Discussion Paper no. 1274.

de la Fuente, A., 1997a, "Innovación y Crecimiento", Report for the COTEC Foundation, Instituto de Análisis Económico, Barcelona.

de la Fuente, A., 1997b, "Fiscal policy and growth in the OECD", mimeo, Instituto de Análisis Económico, Barcelona.

Doménech, R. and J. Boscá, 1996, "A Database for the Analysis of Economic Growth in the OECD, 1960-95", Ministry of Economics and Finance, Dirección Gral. de Planificación, Madrid.

Dowrick, S. and D. T. Nguyen, 1989, "OECD Comparative Economic Growth 1950-85: Catch-up and Convergence", *American Economic Review*, 79 (5), Dec., pp. 1010-1030.

The Economist, "Europe's Tiger Economy: Green is Good", May 17th, 1997.

Fingleton, J., 1996, "Competition Policy in Ireland", mimeo, Trinity College, Dublin.

Giavazzi, F. and M. Pagano, 1990, "Can severe fiscal contraction be expansionary? Tales of two small European Countries", in O. Blanchard and S. Fischer, editors, *NBER Macroeconomics Annual 1990*, Cambridge, MA, MIT Press, pp. 75-110.

Honohan, P., 1992, "Fiscal adjustment in Ireland in the 1980s", *Economic and Social Review* 23(3), pp. 285-315.

Jorgenson, D. W. and K-Y Yun, 1986, "Tax policy and capital allocation", *Scandinavian Journal of Economics* 88(2), pp. 355-77.

Jorgenson, D. W. and K-Y Yun, "Tax reform and US Economic Growth", *Journal of Political Economy* 98(5), 1990, pp. 151-193.

Keating, B., 1995, "Measuring growth", in *Proceedings of the Conference on Measuring Economic Growth,* Dublin, Central Statistics Office and Irish Economic Association.

King, R. G. and S. Rebelo, 1990, "Public Policy and Economic Growth: Developing Neoclassical Implications", *Journal of Political Economy*, 98 (5), pp. 126-150.

Landau, D., 1983, "Government Expenditure and Economic Growth: A Cross-Country Study", *Southern Economic Journal*, 49 (3), pp. 783-792.

Landau, D., 1985, "Government Expenditure and Economic Growth in the Developed Countries: 1952-76", *Public Choice*, 47, 3, pp. 459-477.

Landau, D., 1986, "Government and Economic Growth in the Less Developed Countries: An Empirical Study for 1960-80", *Economic Development and Cultural Change,* 35, pp. 35-75.

Leddin, A. and B. Walsh, 1997, "Economic Stabilization and Recovery: Ireland 1979-96", Paper presented at the conference on "Crecimiento económico en España y en Andalucía", Sevilla, Spain, Feb.

Levine, R. and D. Renelt, 1992, "A Sensitivity Analysis of Cross-Country Growth Regressions", *American Economic Review*, 82 (4), pp. 942-963.

Lichtenberg, F., 1992, "R&D Investment and International Productivity Differences", NBER Working Paper no. 4161.

Mankiw, G., D. Romer and D.Weil, 1992, "A Contribution to the Empirics of Economic Growth", *Quarterly Journal of Economics*, pp. 407-437.

Ó Gráda, C. and K. O'Rourke, 1994, "Irish economic growth, 1945-88", CEPR Discussion Paper no. 975, June.

OECD, *Economic Surveys, Ireland,* Paris, various years.

OECD, 1996, *Statistical Compendium,* electronic data base, Paris.

OECD, *Basic Science and Technology Statistics,* Paris, various years.

Ruane, F. and H. Goerg, 1997, "Reflections on Irish Industrial Policy towards Foreign Direct Investment", mimeo, Trinity College, Dublin.

Summers, R. and A. Heston, 1991, "The Penn World Table (Mark 5): An Expanded Set of International Comparisons, 1950-88", *Quarterly Journal of Economics* CVI(2), pp. 327-368.

UNESCO, *Statistical Yearbook,* Paris, various years.

Walsh, B., 1993, "The contribution of human capital formation to post-war economic growth in Ireland", CEPR Discussion Paper no. 819, July.

Walsh, B., 1996, "Stabilization and Adjustment in a Small Open Economy: Ireland, 1979-95", *Oxford Review of Economic Policy* 12(3), pp. 74-86.

134

INDEX